Love One Another, My Friends

Saint Augustine's Homilies on the First Letter of John

An Abridged English Version
by John Leinenweber

1817

HARPER & ROW, PUBLISHERS, SAN FRANCISCO

New York, Grand Rapids, Philadelphia, St. Louis
London, Singapore, Sydney, Tokyo

To Bruce Allison,
pastor and preacher

FIRST EDITION

Library of Congress Cataloging-in-Publication Data

Augustine, Saint. Bishop of Hippo.
  Love one another, my friends.

  1. Bible. N.T. Epistles of John, 1st — Sermons — Early works to 1800. 2. Love — Sermons — Early works to 1800.
3. Sermons, English—Translations from Latin.
4. Sermons, Latin — Translations into English.
I. Leinenweber, John. II. Title.
BS2805.A85 1989   252′.014   88-45982
ISBN 0-06-065233-0

89 90 91 92 93   HC   10 9 8 7 6 5 4 3 2 1

Contents

Introduction

Homilies is the word I have chosen to translate the Latin name of this work of Augustine's, *Tractatus,* in order to suggest the simplicity of his approach to the first letter of Saint John. Augustine was a bishop, and his friend and earliest biographer, Possidius, tells us that "up to his very last illness he preached the word of God in church incessantly, vigorously, and forcefully, with clear mind and sound judgment." The spiritual welfare of the flock entrusted to him in the out-of-the-way African city of Hippo was his concern. He seldom displays his learning, though neither does he talk down to his listeners. He considers that he is preaching to himself as well as to them.

Unlike modern scholars, who are interested in questions of authorship and the details of when and where a biblical book was written, and who endeavor to discern the development of an author's thought in the work being studied, Augustine just takes the letter line by line, expressing the ideas suggested to him. Some lines pass by with hardly a comment, others are developed at some length, as the Lord moves him to speak. A constant thought with him is that he is not teaching his own doctrine, but passing on to others what the Spirit has given him to say.

In such a case a reader will want to know the character of the preacher, in order to judge how well the message is coming through. Augustine is doubtless the best known and best loved of the Latin Fathers of the Church, owing to his book *Confessions.* He is also one of the most distrusted and hated, owing to some of his opinions, especially those on human sexuality. Baron von Hügel called "lumpers" the people who allow what they do not like to prevent them from seeing the good in a work. No one should feel obliged to agree with Augustine all down the line. He was dealing with the problems of his time, the period of the decline of the Roman Empire, of barbarian invasions, of a divided Church, of the rise of the Pelagian heresy. Some of his solutions—forced baptisms, for instance—are rejected today. But those who have read his *Confessions* will remember his discussions of human and divine love, the spiritual and the material worlds, the nature of evil, sin, memory, and time, and think that however much Augustine's opinions may be conditioned by the period in which he wrote, they are worth reading.

The historical part of his *Confessions* carries us little further than Augustine's baptism, which took place on Easter 387, in Milan. The next year he returned home to Africa and entered into a period of contemplative retirement. In 391 he was ordained a priest—reluctantly, it seems—in Hippo Regius, on the Mediterranean coast, and in 395 he was chosen bishop of that city. He considered himself ill-prepared for the priesthood, especially because of his ignorance of Scripture. As he studied Scripture he issued a stream of biblical commentaries, the most celebrated of which are two series of sermons, on the psalms and on the gospel according to John, which he delivered during the years 414-417.

Augustine seems to have delivered the first twelve of his one hundred and twenty-four homilies on the gospel, in alternation with sermons on the psalms, between December 414 and Easter 415. At Easter, as he tells us in a prologue to the present work (not included in this volume), during the "solemnity of the holy days" it was customary to read certain particular lessons from the gospels every year, and because these could not be changed he interrupted his commentary on John. Searching for another subject on which to speak during Easter week, he decided on the first letter of John: he believed that it was by the same author as the gospel of John; it was a dear and much-honored book; and, most of all, it would speak to his flock of love. "John has said many things, and almost all of them concern love." The first six of the ten homilies were delivered on the days of the Easter octave. But this time proved too short for Augustine to cover the whole of the letter, so he preached four additional homilies later in the spring. Even then he had not completed his discussion, and he seems never to have done so.

I have broken up the ten homilies into shorter chapters, and given them titles that express the central ideas of the chapters; for example, The Commandment of Love, Two Loves (of God and of the world), Christ and the Antichrists, Unanswered Prayer, Love of Our Enemies, God First Loved Us, and so on. This short list will suggest some of the themes that Augustine deals with: the world (so important in John's writings), prayer, our enemies, fear of God, the Church. His is in large part moral teaching: What does one actually do to love God and to love one's sister and brother? What are the pitfalls of loving? How does one learn to love more? Everywhere evident as well is his great desire for eternal life with God. The homiletic form does not allow Augustine to create a synthetic work, yet many of his richest and most rewarding ideas pass by during the course of these homilies.

* * *

The passages in John's first letter on which Augustine is commenting have been italicized in the text. Other quotations are distinguished by quotation marks when they are fairly exact (note that he does not always quote a passage in precisely the same words), and these and other allusions are identified in notes at the end of this volume. Quotations and allusions in their English form are based on the Revised Standard and Rheims-Douai versions of the Bible.

Three Latin words are used throughout the homilies: *amor, caritas,* and *dilectio,* all of which mean "love." One might lament the poverty of the English language, except that Augustine seems to have used the three synonymously. In this he relies on the example of Scripture (his Latin version), which, he says, does not intend any distinction among the three (see *City of God,* XIV, 7).

I have used the Latin text published, with a French translation, by Paul Agaësse, S. J., in the series "Sources chrétiennes" (no. 75), *Commentaire de la Première Épître de S. Jean* (Paris, 1984). Agaësse says that this reproduces the text published in the Latin patrology of Migne (vol. 35, 1977–2062), which, with the exception of two variants, is that of the Benedictines of Saint-Maur.

I know of two earlier translations of these homilies on 1 John, a complete one in the "Select Library of the Nicene and Post-Nicene Fathers" (first series, volume VII, 1888; reprint, Grand Rapids, 1956), and an abridged one by John Burnaby (author of a celebrated study of Augustine, *Amor Dei*), which is included in Volume VIII of the "Library of Christian Classics" (London, 1955) entitled *Augustine: Later Works.* The seventh homily is included in *Augustine of Hippo: Selected Writings* in the Paulist Press "Classics of Western Spirituality" series (New York, Paulist, 1984).

I want to thank John Watkins for reading this version of the homilies and for suggesting revisions and corrections; and Bruce Allison, Deborah and David Douglas, Barbara Faris, Benedict Neenan, and Aelred Seton Shanley for their help and encouragement. Most of the work on this book was done at the Monastery of Christ in the Desert, Abiquiu, New Mexico. Thanks are also due to Florence Aebersold, who was kind enough to type the final version.

* * *

At the end of his introduction to the homilies, John Burnaby remarks that

Augustine's exegesis is often unsatisfactory, and his arguments on the text of Scripture are often forced. . . . But if he is an indifferent exegete, he is an incomparable preacher. These homilies show him at the summit of his extraordinary power to move the soul.

These sentences may serve as a warning to a modern reader not to compare Augustine to the biblical scholars of our own time. Gerald Bonner, in the essay on Augustine in *The Cambridge History of the Bible,* says that "for Augustine, it is not so much the words of the Bible themselves as the doctrine underlying the word which is important." In this connection he quotes Augustine's own words:

It is the duty of the interpreter and teacher of holy scripture, the defender of the true faith and the opponent of error, both to teach what is right and to refute what is wrong, and in the performance of this task to conciliate the hostile, to rouse the careless, and to tell the ignorant both what is occurring at present and what is probable in the future.

The reader of these homilies will find Augustine teaching what he takes to be Christian doctrine, as the words of Saint John's letter inspire him, and as God gives him strength and understanding.

1. The Incarnation
(1 John 1:1–4)

That which was from the beginning, which we have heard, which we have seen with our eyes and our hands have touched, concerning the Word of life. How could anyone have touched the Word if it had not become flesh and dwelt among us? This Word that became flesh to be touched by our hands began to be flesh in Mary's womb. But the Word didn't begin to exist then, because John says of it that it *was from the beginning.* See if the gospel doesn't confirm the letter—his gospel begins, "In the beginning was the Word, and the Word was with God."

Is there anyone who will take the phrase *Word of life* as an expression used to designate Christ, and not as his body, which was touched by human hands? See what comes next: *And life itself was made manifest.* Christ is then the Word of life. And how was life made manifest? It was *from the beginning,* but it wasn't manifest to human beings. It was manifest to angels, who saw it and ate it as their bread. Scripture says that "men have eaten the bread of angels." And so *life itself was made manifest in the flesh.* This manifestation took place so that our eyes might see something that only hearts could see, and in this way our hearts might be healed. Only hearts could see the Word. Our bodily eyes could see the flesh but not the Word. "The Word became flesh," which we could see, to heal our hearts, which could see the Word.

And we saw it, and testify to it. Where did we see it? We saw it in its manifestation. That means that we saw it in this visible light that comes from the sun. What made it possible to see the sun's Maker in the sun's light? The psalm tells us that "he placed his tabernacle in the sun; and, like a bridegroom coming out of his bridal chamber, he rejoiced as a giant to run his course." The sun's Maker existed before there was a sun or a morning star or any of the constellations; he existed before any of the angels; he is the true Creator, because "everything was made by him and without him nothing was made." "He placed his tabernacle in the sun" so that we could see him with the eyes with which we look at the sun; he showed us his flesh by manifesting it in this earthly light. His "bridal chamber" was the Virgin's womb, because it was there that the bridegroom and bride were united, the bridegroom being the Word and his flesh the bride. It is written in the book of Genesis that "they shall be two in one flesh," and in the gospel the Lord says, "So they are no longer two but one flesh." But it is Isaiah who expresses this best when he says in the name of Christ, "He has wreathed me as a bridegroom, and as a bride he has adorned me with jewels." One person is speaking, claiming to be both bridegroom and bride. There are not two but one flesh, because "the Word became flesh and dwelt among us."

We testify to it, and proclaim to you the eternal life which was with the Father and was made manifest to us—among us, or *to us. That which we have seen and heard we proclaim to you.* They saw the Lord himself present in his flesh; and they heard the words that came from his mouth, and they proclaimed them to us. We too have heard his words, but we haven't seen him. Are we less fortunate than those who both saw and heard? If that were so why would he add, *so that you too may have communion with us?* They saw; we haven't seen. But even so we are sharers with them, because we have the same faith. One of the disciples didn't believe even when he saw. He said that he wouldn't believe unless he put his fingers in the place of the nails and touched Jesus' wounds. At that moment Jesus allowed human hands to touch him—the one who lets angels behold him always! And the disciple felt him and cried out, "My Lord and my God!" Because he touched a man he acknowledged God. And to console us who can't touch one now seated in heaven, but who can reach him by faith, the Lord told him, "You have believed because you have seen me; blessed are those who do not see and who believe." He is pointing to us, describing us! Let us experience this blessedness! Let us hold firmly what we do not see, because those who saw have proclaimed it.

So that you too, John says, *may have communion with us.* Is this so much—communion with other human beings? Don't belittle it. See what he adds: *And our communion may be with God the Father and with his son Jesus Christ. And these things,* he says, *we write to you that your joy may be full.* In that fellowship, that love, that unity, our joy is full; that is what he is saying.

2. Walk in the Light
(1 John 1:5–2:2)

And this is the message we have heard from him and proclaim to you.
What is it? They saw, they touched the Word of life with their
hands. God's only Son, who was from the beginning, became
for a while visible and palpable. For what purpose did he come?
What did he make known to us that was new? What did he
wish to teach? Why did he do what he did—the Word becom-
ing flesh, God who is over all things suffering what he did not
deserve and accepting blows from hands he himself had made?
Let us listen: for if the teaching doesn't bear fruit, then the re-
port of what happened—that Christ was born, that he suffered—is only a diversion for the mind and not a support.
What momentous thing do you hear?

Listen: *God is light,* he says, *and in him is no darkness at all.* He
speaks of light, but his words are obscure. May the light he has
spoken of so illumine our hearts that we may come to understand his words! This is what we proclaim: that *God is light, and
in him is no darkness at all.*

Who would dare to say that there is darkness in God? Or to
ask what that light is, or the darkness? These questions apply to
what our eyes can see. *God is light,* someone says—and so are
the sun and the moon, so are lamps. There must exist something far greater than these, far more extraordinary, something
that far surpasses them. To the extent that God is beyond what
he has created, that a maker is beyond what he has made, that
wisdom is beyond what is made by wisdom, so also must this
light be far beyond all things.

And perhaps we will come near it if we can recognize what
this light is, and if we devote ourselves to it so that we are illumined by it. Of ourselves we are darkness; but if we are illu-

mined by that light we can be light. And it doesn't bring shame upon us, because we do this for ourselves. Who are they who are ashamed of themselves? It's those who recognize that they are sinners. And who are not put to shame by the light? It's those who are illumined by it. What does it mean, to be illumined by the light? Those who see themselves darkened by their sins, but desire to be illumined by the light, draw near to it. That is why the psalm tells us, "Draw near to him and be illumined, and your faces will not be ashamed." The light won't shame you if, when it shows you that you are foul and deformed, these things displease you. Then you may perceive the beauty of the light. This is what John wants to teach us.

Again, if *God is light, and in him is no darkness at all,* and if we must have communion with him, then darkness must be driven out of us, because darkness can have no communion with light. You have the words of the apostle Paul too: "What communion has light with darkness?" And so ask yourself now, "What shall I do? How will I become light? I am living in sin and iniquity. Despair and sadness are stealing into me. There is salvation only in communion with God." *God is light, and in him is no darkness at all.* Sins are darkness. It is the Apostle who tells us that the devil and his angels are the rulers of this present darkness, and he wouldn't call them rulers of darkness unless they were the rulers of sinners, the ones who dominate the wicked.

What are we to do, my friends? We must have communion with God, because that is our only hope of life eternal. But our iniquities are dark, and they press upon us so that we cannot have communion with God. What hope have we then? Didn't I promise that I would say something during these days to bring you gladness? If I don't, there is only sadness. *God is light, and in him is no darkness at all.* What will become of us?

Let us listen. Perhaps John will console us; perhaps he will lift us up and give us hope so that we will not falter on our way. We are running, running toward our home. If we despair of reaching it, it is by our despair that we fail. God wants us to reach it. In order to have us there with him he nourishes us on the way. And so let us listen: *If we say that we have communion with him and we walk in darkness, we lie and do not practice the truth.* Let us not say that we have communion with him if we are walking in darkness. *But if we walk in the light, as he is in the light, we have communion with one another.* So let us walk in the light, as he is in the light, so that we may have communion with him.

But what are we to do about our sins? Listen to what follows: *and the blood of Jesus his Son will cleanse us from all offense.* God has taken all our anxiety from us. It is right for us to celebrate the Passover in which the Lord's blood, which cleanses us from all offense, was poured out. Let us be at peace! The devil held a "bond of servitude" against us, but it has been canceled by the blood of Christ. *The blood of Jesus his Son will cleanse us,* he says, *from all offense.*

What does it mean to say *from all offense?* Those newly baptized, whom we call infants, have been cleansed from all their sins in Christ's name, and by the blood of him they have now acknowledged. They came in old, they went out young, as infants. Their old life was a deterioration, their new life is a regeneration. But what of us? Our past sins have been pardoned too, not just theirs. But after all of our sins have been pardoned and abolished, as we live among the temptations of this world, perhaps we contract others. Let us then do what we can: let us confess what we are, so that the One who is always what he is may heal us.

For see what is said next: *If we say we have no sin we deceive ourselves and the truth is not in us.* Therefore if you confess that you are a sinner, the truth is in you. The truth itself is light. Your life does not yet have its perfect splendor because there are sins in it, but you have begun to be illumined because there is confession of sins in it. See what follows: *If we confess our offenses, he is faithful and just in forgiving us our offenses and in cleansing us from all unrighteousness.* We confess not just our past sins but all those we contract from this life. No one can exist in this flesh without some light sins at least. But you shouldn't think lightly of those sins we call light. If you think lightly of them when you weigh them, be afraid when you count them! Many light objects make one huge one; many drops fill a river; many grains make a heap.

And what hope have we? Before everything else there is confession of sins, lest one of us reckon himself to be righteous and raise his nose in the air before God, who sees what he is, this person who once didn't even exist. Before everything else, then, confession. And then love. What do they say of it? "Love buries a multitude of sins."

Now let us see whether John isn't enjoining us to love because faults come upon us while we are unaware, and it is only love that destroys them. Pride destroys love and so we can say that humility strengthens it. Love destroys our faults. Humility pertains to the confession we make when we confess that we are sinners. This is true humility; not the words we say when we are afraid that we'll antagonize people by our conceit if we describe ourselves as righteous. Tell people what you are and tell God what you are. If you don't tell God what you really are, he'll condemn what he finds in you. If you don't want this to happen, then condemn yourself. Do you want him to forgive you? Then acknowledge what you are and say to him, "Turn away your face from my sins." Say this to him, too, from the same psalm: "for I know my unrighteousness."

If we confess our offenses, he is faithful and just in forgiving us our offenses and in cleansing us from all unrighteousness. If we say we have not sinned we make him a liar and his word is not in us. If you say you haven't sinned, you are making him a liar while attempting to make a truthful person of yourself. But how can God be a liar and a human being truthful when Scripture tells us just the opposite when it says, "Every person is a liar; God alone is true." And so God is true in himself; it is through him that you are true, because in yourself you are a liar.

Do you think that John is promising you that you won't be punished for your sins when he says that God *is faithful and just in cleansing us from all unrighteousness?* Do you think you can say to yourself, "Let's sin, let's do what we want without anxiety, because Christ cleanses us, he is faithful and just, and he cleanses us from all unrighteousness"? John takes away from you a vicious security and instills a profitable fear. Is it a vicious security you want? Be solicitous! *He is faithful and just in forgiving us our offenses,* if we are always dissatisfied with ourselves and are willing to change so long as we are not perfect.

And so what follows? *My little children, I am writing this to you so that you may not sin.* But suppose that sin steals up on you out of your human situation? What will happen then? Should you despair? Listen: *and if any one does sin, we have an advocate with the Father, Jesus Christ the righteous; and he is the one who makes expiation for our sins.* And so he is our advocate. Live so that you don't sin, but if some sin steals up on you out of the circumstances of your life, look at it right away, regret it, condemn it; and when you've condemned your sin you'll come to your Judge without anxiety. There you have an advocate. Don't be afraid of losing your case, which you have confessed. Sometimes in affairs of this life people entrust themselves to an eloquent speaker and are saved. You are entrusting yourself to the Word, and will you be lost? Of course not. So shout out: *We have an advocate with the Father!*

And see how John himself preserves his humility. He was a great and righteous man; he drank the secrets of the mysteries from the Lord's breast. From Christ's breast he drank in the mystery of his divinity, so that he could write, "In the beginning was the Word, and the Word was with God." This great man didn't say that *you* have an advocate with the Father, he said *we* have. He chose to include himself among sinners, so that he would have Christ as his advocate. Friends, it is Jesus Christ the righteous one whom we have as our advocate with the Father; he is the expiation for our sins.

But someone will ask, "Don't the saints intercede for us? Don't the bishops and leaders in the Church intercede for the people?" But look in the Scriptures and see that the leaders also recommend that they themselves be included in the prayers of people. Paul writes to the Colossians: "Pray for us also." The Apostle prays for the people and they pray for him. I pray for you, my friends, and you too, please pray for me. Let all members pray for one another, and let our Head intercede for us all!

Don't be surprised, then, that John goes on to shut the mouths of those who divide God's church, who would detach themselves and say, "Lo, here is the Christ!" or, "There he is!" who want to exhibit in a part the one who gained the whole and possesses the whole. When he has said that *he is the . . . expiation for our sins,* John immediately adds, *and not for ours only but also for those of the whole world.* It is certain that "we have found it in the fields of the woods," we have found the Church in every nation, we find the Church throughout the whole world. Don't follow those who pretend to make others righteous but who really cut off parts of the whole. Belong to that mountain which has filled the whole Earth, because Christ *is the . . . expiation for our sins, and not for ours only but also for those of the whole world,* which he purchased with his own blood.

3. The Commandment of Love (1 John 2:3–11)

And in this, John says, *we know him, if we keep his commandments.* What commandments are these? *One who says that he knows him and does not keep his commandments is a liar and the truth is not in him.* You ask again, What commandments are these? John says that *whoever keeps his word, truly in this one, love of God is perfected.* Let us see whether this commandment isn't called love. We asked, What commandments? And he said, *Whoever keeps his word, truly in this one love of God is perfected.* Refer to the gospel and see if this isn't the commandment. "A new commandment," Jesus says there, "I give you, that you love one another." *By this we know that we are in him, if in him we are perfect.* Perfect in love is what he means. What is the perfection of love? It is to love our enemies, and to love them to this end: that they may be our sisters and brothers.

Our love shouldn't be unspiritual. It's fine to wish someone good health; but even if that's lacking, may the soul be safe! Do you pray for your friend's life? That's good. Do you rejoice in your enemy's death? That's bad. Maybe the life you wish for your friend is unprofitable, and your enemy's death, that you are happy about, is the best thing for him. You can't be sure whether this life is profitable to someone; but that true life which is with God is beyond any doubt profitable. Love your enemies in this way: that you want them to be your sisters and brothers, that you would call them into communion with you.

This is how Jesus loved. When he was hanging on the cross he didn't say, "Father, give them long life; they are putting me to death, but let them live." What did he ask? "Forgive them, for they know not what they do." It was eternal death he was thrusting away from them; he was doing it by his prayer, which is full of mercy, and his surpassing power. Many of them believed and their shedding of Christ's blood was forgiven them. First they shed it in rage, and then they drank it in faith. *By this we know that we are in him, if in him we are perfect.* Our Lord is inviting us to this perfection which consists in loving our enemies when he says, "Be perfect, therefore, as your heavenly Father is perfect."

And so *one who says he abides in him,* in Christ, *ought to walk in the same way in which he walked.* And how did he walk, my friends? What is John teaching us? Does he want us to walk on the sea? Not at all. It's this: that we walk in the way of righteousness. And what way is that? I have already reminded you of it. Even when he was fastened to the cross he walked in this way, which is the way of love. "Father, forgive them, for they know not what they do." If you have learned to pray for your enemies, you are walking in the way of the Lord.

Dearly beloved, I am writing you no new commandment but an old commandment which you had from the beginning. What commandment was John calling old? It's the one *which you had,* he says, *from the beginning.* It's old, then, in the sense that you have already heard it. And it is new: "A new commandment I give you, that you love one another." John shows how this commandment is also new when he says, *Again it is a new commandment I am writing to you.* It's not some other commandment but the very one he has called old that is also new. Why is this? Because it is one *which is true in him and in you.* Why is it old? Because you already know it. And why is it new? *Because the darkness has passed and the true light is already shining.* This is what makes it new: that darkness pertains to the old nature and light to the new. What is it Paul tells us? "You have put off the old nature and have put on the new." And what else does he say? "Once you were darkness, but now you are light in the Lord."

One who says he is in the light. . . . Now John is making his thought plain. *One who says he is in the light and hates his brother is in the darkness even until now.* Friends, how long must I keep telling you, love your enemies? See that you don't do what is much worse and hate your own sisters and brothers! If these are the only people you love, you aren't perfect yet; but what are you if you hate them? Where does that put you? Look into your own hearts. Don't keep up hatred against your sisters and brothers for any hard word or for any quarrel on earth. No one who hates sister or brother can claim to walk in the light, no one can claim to walk in Christ. *One who says he is in the light and hates his brother is in the darkness even until now.*

One who loves his brother abides in the light, and there is no cause for stumbling in him. Who are the people who themselves stumble or cause stumbling in others? It's those who stumble over Christ or his Church. Why is it that there is no cause for stumbling in those who love their sister or brother? It's because those who love their sister or brother bear everything for the sake of unity, and because it is in the unity of love that brotherly or sisterly love exists. You are offended by someone—someone wicked or someone you suppose is wicked or someone you pretend is wicked: will you separate yourself from so many who are good? If you loved your sisters and brothers, there would be no stumbling for you. Listen to what the psalmist says: "Great peace have those who love your law; nothing can make them stumble." Who are the people the psalmist says do not stumble or cause stumbling in others? It is those who love God's law, those who are firm in love. But someone will object that the psalmist spoke of those who love God's law, not of those who love their sisters and brothers. Listen to what the Lord says: "A new commandment I give you, that you love one another." What is a law if not a commandment? And how is it that they don't stumble if it isn't that they put up with one another, forbear one another as Paul says: "forbearing one another in love, eager to maintain the unity of the Spirit in the bond of peace"? And this is Christ's law, as Paul says in another place: "Bear one another's burdens," he says, "and thus you will fulfill the law of Christ."

One who hates his brother walks in the darkness and does not know where he is going because the darkness has blinded his eyes. Who is as blind as those who hate their sisters and brothers? To prove this to you: they've stumbled against a mountain! Isn't Christ that "stone cut out of the mountain without hands," Christ who came from the kingdom of the Jews without a man taking part in his conception? Isn't this how we present the Church, my friends? Hasn't the Church reached every nation? Hasn't the promise made to Abraham so many years ago, that in his posterity all nations would be blessed, been fulfilled? This was promised to one believer, and a multitude of believers fills the world! See in this the mountain covering the whole face of the earth. See in this the city of which it was said, "A city set on a mountain cannot be hid." But people stumble on the mountain. When they are told to go up the mountain they say, "There is no mountain," and they dash their heads against it instead of seeking a dwelling place there.

Dear friends, what is more conspicuous than a mountain? But there are mountains that we don't know because they are situated in some other part of the earth. Which of you knows Mount Olympus? And people who dwell there don't know our mountains. These mountains are in different parts of the earth. But that is not true of the Mountain that covers the whole face of the earth. Who can get lost there? Who can break his skull by stumbling against it? Is there anyone who doesn't know the "city set on a mountain"? But don't be surprised that those who hate their sisters and brothers don't know it, because they walk in darkness; they don't know where they're going because the darkness has blinded their eyes. They don't see the mountain.

4. I Am Writing to You
(1 John 2:12–14)

I am writing to you, little children, because your sins are forgiven you through his name. John calls them "little children," because the forgiveness of sins is a birth. But through whose name is it that your sins are forgiven? My name—Augustine? No, and not through Paul or Peter either. There are people who would divide the Church for their own purposes, who are trying to fracture our unity. To them the Apostle's love is a fruitful mother— she shows her heart, she tears her breast, so to speak, by her words, she weeps over the children she sees come forth only for burial, she calls back to a single name those who want to give themselves many names, she turns love away from herself toward Christ, and she asks: "Was it Paul who was crucified for you? Were you baptized in the name of Paul?" What she is saying is, "I don't want you to belong to me; I want you to belong *along with* me, all of us belonging to the One who died for us, who was crucified for us." And so John says here, *your sins are forgiven you through* Christ's *name,* not through any mere human's name.

I am writing to you, fathers. Why did he write to the children first? *Because your sins are forgiven you through his name,* and because you have been reborn to a new life. That is why you are children. And why did he write to mothers and fathers? *Because you know him who is from the beginning:* "the beginning" is related to parenthood. Christ is new in his flesh but ancient in his divinity. How ancient do you reckon he is? How many years old? Do you think he is older than his mother? Surely he is, for "all things were made through him." If everything was made through him, then because he was ancient he made the mother who bore him as one new; and because he was ancient he existed even before his mother's ancestors. One of his mother's ancestors was Abraham, and the Lord said, "Before Abraham was I am." Only before Abraham? Heaven and earth were made before there was any human being, and before them was the Lord—*is* the Lord, rather.

It was entirely right that he said, "Before Abraham was I *am*," and not, "Before Abraham I *was*." If we say of something that it *was*, then it no longer *is*; and if we say that it *will be*, then it doesn't yet exist. Christ knows only existence. Because he is God he knows only *is*, he doesn't know *was* or *will be*. In him there is only a single day, but it is an eternal day. It doesn't fall between yesterday and tomorrow, because when yesterday is over today begins, and today will end with the coming tomorrow. There isn't any darkness in that day or any night, no intervals or proportions or hours. Call it whatever you like: a day, if you like that, or a year; or years, because the psalm says of it that "your years shall have no end." When was it called a day? When it was said to the Lord, "Today I have begotten you." He was begotten by the eternal Father, begotten from eternity, begotten in eternity, without any beginning, with no bounds, no intervals in his existence. This is because he is what he is, because he is "he who is." He told Moses that this was his name. "You shall tell them: He who is has sent me to you."

But why should we say, "before Abraham" or "before Noah" or "before Adam"? Listen to Scripture: "Before the daystar have I begotten you." Ultimately he was before heaven and earth. And why? Because "everything was made through him and without him nothing was made." And so, mothers and fathers, acknowledge him. You came to be mothers and fathers by acknowledging "that which is from the beginning."

I am writing to you, young men. He calls them *children, fathers, young men*—children because they are born; mothers and fathers because they acknowledge the one who is "the Beginning"; but why young women and men? *Because you have overcome the evil one.* There is birth in the children, antiquity in the mothers and fathers, strength in the young women and men. If the evil one is overcome by the young women and men, then it is the evil one that is fighting against us, that assaults us but doesn't take us by assault. And why not? Is it because we are strong? Or is it because he is strong in us, the One who was weak in the hands of his persecutors? The One who didn't resist his persecutors has made us strong. "He was crucified in weakness but he lives by the power of God."

I am writing to you, children. Why are they children? *Because you have known the Father. I am writing to you, fathers,* he says again, *because you know him who is from the beginning.* You must remember that you are mothers and fathers. If you forget *him who is from the beginning,* you have lost your parenthood. *I am writing to you, young men.* You must consider over and over again that you are young women and men: fight so as to conquer; conquer that you may be crowned in victory; be humble so that you don't fall in the fighting. I *am writing to you, young men, because you are strong, and the word of God abides in you, and you have overcome the evil one.*

All these things, dear friends—that we have known that which is in the beginning, that we are strong, that we have known the Father—don't all of these commend to us a kind of knowledge and commend to us love as well? What John is saying is that if we have known, then let us love! Knowledge without love doesn't save anyone. "Knowledge puffs up, love builds up." If you have in mind to confess the truth without love, then you are starting to resemble demons. The demons acknowledged God's Son and asked, "What have you to do with us?" And Christ drove them away. You must acknowledge him and also embrace him. They were afraid of him because of their misdeeds; you must love the one who pardons your misdeeds!

5. Two Loves
(1 John 2:15–17)

How is it possible for us to love God if we love the world? God indeed makes us capable of being inhabited by love. But there are two loves: the love of the world and the love of God. If we are full of love of the world, there is no way the love of God can enter us. So we must allow our love of the world to give ground and let the love of God inhabit us; we must allow the better one a place in us. You used to love the world, but don't love it any longer! When you've drawn earthly love out of your heart, you'll draw in divine love. Divine love is already beginning to dwell in you, and no evil can come from divine love. Listen now to John's words—what he wants to do is purify us. He finds the human heart like a field, but in what condition is the field? If he finds a forest there, he clears it; if he finds it cleared, he plants it. His desire is to plant a tree there, and the tree is love. What is the forest he wants to clear? It is love of the world. Listen to the words of this one who clears the forest: *Do not love the world*—this is the next verse of his letter—*or the things in the world. If anyone loves the world, the love of the Father is not in him.*

You've heard that *if anyone loves the world, the love of the Father is not in him.* Dear friends, don't say in your hearts that this is wrong. It is God who says it. The Holy Spirit has spoken through the apostle John. There is nothing more true: *If anyone loves the world, the love of the Father in not in him.* Do you want to possess the love of the Father, and through this be a coheir with his Son? Then don't love the world. Shut out love of the world, so that you can be filled by the love of God. You're full now—pour out what you have in you, so that you can be filled with what you don't have!

We can be sure that our sisters and brothers have been reborn of water and the Spirit. A few years ago I too was reborn of water and the Spirit. It's good for us not to love the world; otherwise, the sacraments lead to our condemnation instead of being the means of our salvation. The way of salvation is to possess love's root; it's to possess the "power of religion," not just its "appearance." The appearance is good and holy, but what is it worth if it has no root? A branch that's cut off, isn't it thrown into the fire? Possess the appearance, but an appearance that is attached to its root. How can you be so rooted as not to be rooted up? It's by holding firm to love, being, in Paul's words, "rooted and grounded in love." How is love going to take root in ground so dense with love of the world? You have to clear the forest! It's a mighty seed you are to sow; don't leave anything in the field to choke it out. These are clearing words: *Do not love the world or the things in the world. If anyone loves the world, the love of the Father is not in him.*

For all that is in the world is the lust of the flesh and the lust of the eyes and the pride of life (John mentions three things), *which are not of the Father but of the world. And the world passes away, and its lusts; but one who does the will of God abides forever, for God himself abides forever.*

Why shouldn't I love what God has made? Which do you prefer: to love the things of time and to pass away with time, or not to love the world and to live forever with God? The river of temporal things draws us along; but our lord Jesus Christ was like a tree by the river's edge. He became flesh, he died, he arose, he ascended into heaven. He willed to plant himself, so to speak, by the river of temporal things. Are you being rushed along toward treacherous rapids? Hold on to the tree! Is love of the world whirling you on? Hold fast to Christ! For your sake he became subject to time; he became temporal to make you eternal. When he too became temporal, it was in such a way that he remained eternal. He took something from time, but he didn't take away from eternity. You were born temporal and became subject to time through sin; he became subject to time through mercy in order to pardon your sins.

What a difference there is between two people in prison when one is a criminal and the other his visitor! Sometimes a person goes to visit a friend, and both are seen to be in prison, but their conditions are very distinct and different! One is held fast by his situation, the other brought there by his human sympathies. So were we held in our mortal state by guilt; Christ came down in mercy, he came to the captive as a redeemer, not an oppressor. The Lord poured out his own blood for us, he redeemed us, he altered our hope. We still bear death in our bodies and take our future immortality on trust; while we are being tossed about on the sea, we have already fixed our anchor of hope on land.

So let us not *love the world or the things in the world.* The things in the world are *the lust of the flesh and the lust of the eyes and the pride of life*: three things.

Don't anyone say, *"the things in the world . . .* why, God made them! He made heaven and earth, the sea, the sun and moon, the stars. He made everything in the heavens. He made everything the sea contains, all the things on earth, those that creep, animals, trees, those that fly. These are *things in the world* and God made them. Why shouldn't I love what God has made?"

May you have God's Spirit to show you that all these things are good, but it is a mistake for you to love the creatures and abandon their Creator. They seem beautiful to you, but how much more beautiful is the One who formed them! Dear friends, be aware of this. Don't let Satan steal up on you, saying the things typical of him, such as, "Enjoy everything God has made! Why has he made them if not for you to enjoy?" People get intoxicated by this and are ruined and forget their Creator. When they use the things he has made avidly and immoderately, they are snubbing him. Paul says of people like this that "they worshipped and served the creature rather than the Creator, who is blessed forever." God doesn't forbid you to love these things, but he doesn't want you to value them as the source of your happiness. Rather, he wants you to approve and praise them in order for you to love him who is their Creator.

It's as if a bridegroom were to give a ring to his bride, and she came to value the ring more than the one who gave it. By all means let her love the bridegroom's gift, but if she were to say, "The ring's enough for me, I don't want to see his face," what sort of woman would this be? Who wouldn't consider her an adulteress in her heart? The reason a bridegroom gives a pledge is to be loved in his pledge. Well then, God gave you all these things, so love him who made them! There's something more that he wants to give you: he wants to give you himself, who made these things. Even though they are made by God, if you love them and you disregard him and love the world, won't your love be counted adulterous?

All those who love the world John calls *world*. These are the only three things they have, *the lust of the flesh and the lust of the eyes and the pride of life*. They only want to eat, to drink, to have sex with each other, to give themselves to pleasures of this kind. Does this mean that there is no proper place for these things? Or when we are told not to love them, does this mean we shouldn't eat or drink or produce children? This isn't what is meant. But there should be moderation in your use of them, on account of the Creator, so that you are not encumbered by your love of them.

You are put to the test in this regard only when two things are proposed to you, and you have to choose one or the other. Do you desire righteousness or gain? What if you haven't anything to live on, neither food nor drink, and you can get them only by sin? Isn't it better for you to love what lasts than to commit sin? Financial gain you can see; you don't see the loss of your faith. This, John says, is *the lust of the flesh,* the inordinate desire for things that pertain only to the body, such as food and sexual pleasures and so on.

And the lust of the eyes: this is what John calls inquisitiveness, a foolish or dangerous desire to know things. There are so many kinds! This is what is at work in shows and spectacles, in diabolical rites, in magic, in sorceries: inquisitiveness. Sometimes it even tempts God's servants in such a way that they want to do something that will seem miraculous; they want to test whether God hears them. This is inquisitiveness, it is *lust of the eyes,* it is *not of the Father.* If God gives you the power, go ahead and perform a miracle; that's why he gives you that power. But it is wrong to say that people who don't perform miracles won't be part of God's kingdom. What did the Lord tell his apostles when they were rejoicing that demons were subject to them? "Do not rejoice in this . . . but rejoice that your names are written in heaven." He would have you and the apostles rejoice in the same thing. It is a terrible thing for you if your name is not written in heaven. Is it a terrible thing for you if you don't raise the dead? Or if you don't walk on the sea? Or if you don't cast out demons? If you've received the power of doing these things, use it humbly, not proudly, for the Lord has said that certain false prophets will perform signs and wonders. Therefore keep away from *the pride of life. The pride of life* is simply pride. We like to boast of our honors; we think we're great because of our riches or some power we have.

You won't find anything by which human cupidity is tempted except these three things: *the lust of the flesh, and the lust of the eyes and the pride of life.* By these three the Lord was tempted by the devil. He was tempted by *the lust of the flesh* when the devil said to him, "If you are the Son of God, command these stones to become loaves of bread"; this happened when he was hungry after his fast. How did he repel the tempter and at the same time teach us his soldiers how we are to fight? Listen to what he told him: "Man does not live by bread alone but by every word of God."

He was also tempted by *the lust of the eyes.* It was to perform a miracle that the devil urged him, "Throw yourself down; for it is written: He has given his angels charge over you, that they bear you up lest you strike your foot against a stone." He resisted his tempter, for to perform a miracle would have seemed either to be yielding or to be acting out of curiosity. In fact, he did perform miracles; but he did them when he chose, as God and as one healing the sick. If he'd performed a miracle at that time, people would have thought he only wanted to do something strange and wonderful. See what he replied to keep them from thinking this (and when you are so tempted, say it in your turn): "Get behind me Satan; for it is written: You shall not tempt the Lord your God." In other words, "If I do this, I shall be tempting God." The Lord said what he wants you to say. When the enemy says to you, "What kind of person, what kind of Christian are you? Have you ever done even one miracle? Or by your prayers have you raised the dead? Or have you healed the sick?" Answer and say, "It is written: 'You shall not tempt the Lord your God.' I won't tempt him—as if I'll belong to him if I do a miracle and I won't belong to him if I don't! Should I forget his words: 'Rejoice that your names are written in heaven?' "

In what way was the Lord tempted by the *pride of life*? It happened when the devil carried him up to a high place and said to him, "All these I will give you if you will fall down and worship me." By the grandeur of an earthly kingdom he intended to tempt the king of all worlds! But the Lord who made heaven and earth spurned the devil. Was this so remarkable, that Satan was overcome by the Lord? To teach you what you are to answer him, he replied, "It is written: You shall worship the Lord your God, and him only shall you serve."

If you keep to these words, you won't long for the world; and if you don't long for the world, you won't be subject to *the lust of the flesh* or *the lust of the eyes* or *the pride of life*. You will have a place ready to receive love when it comes, so that you can love God. Where there is love of the world, there is no love of God. Hold fast to the love of God. Then, as God is eternal, you too may abide forever. Each person is as his love is. Is it earth that you love? You'll be earth. Is it God? What shall I say? Will you be God? I wouldn't say it on my own, but let us listen to Scripture: "I have said, You are gods and children of the Most High." If this is what you want, to be "gods and children of the Most High," don't love the world or the things in the world. If anyone loves the world, the love of the Father isn't in that one, because everything in the world is *the lust of the flesh and the lust of the eyes and the pride of life.* These are not of the Father but of the world, of the people who love the world. *And the world passes away, and its lusts, but one who does the will of God abides forever, as God himself abides forever.*

6. Christ and the Antichrists (1 John 2:18-23)

Children, it is the last hour. In this passage John is urging children to hurry and grow up, because it is the last hour. Your body's age isn't affected by your will. In a physical sense no one grows when he wills it any more than anyone is born when he wills it. But in a case where birth can be willed, so can growth. No one "is born of water and the Spirit" unless he wills it, and so one who wills it increases and one who does not will it decreases. What does *increase* mean? It means progress. And what does *decrease* mean? It means regress. Have you learned that you've been born? Then recognize that you're a child, a mere baby, and cling eagerly to your mother's breasts and grow up quickly. Your mother is the Church, and her breasts are the two testaments of the Bible. Suck from these testaments her milk, the sacraments we carry out in time for our eternal salvation. When you have been nourished and strengthened by this milk, you'll be capable of eating solid food, this food: "In the beginning was the Word, and the Word was with God, and the Word was God." Christ in his lowly state is our milk; our solid food is the same Christ in his equality with the Father. In order to feed you with bread, he first suckles you with milk. To touch Jesus spiritually with your heart is to know that he is equal to the Father.

This is why Jesus forbade Mary Magdalen to touch him. He told her, "Do not touch me, for I have not yet ascended to the Father." But what's happening here? Did he allow the disciples to touch him and not Mary? Isn't he the same person who told the doubting disciple, "Put your finger here and feel my wounds"? Had he already ascended to the Father? Then why did he forbid Mary to touch him? Shall we answer that he was afraid to have a woman touch him but not a man? But it's by touching him that every one is purified! Was he afraid to be touched by women when they were the ones he chose to manifest himself to first? Wasn't it women who announced his resurrection to the men? In this way the serpent was overcome by his own craft working in reverse: by a woman the devil sent a message of death to the first man, and by a woman the message of life was brought to men.

Why then didn't Christ want to be touched, unless it was because he wanted us to understand that there is a touch that is spiritual? A pure heart touches spiritually, and so a person who understands that Christ is the Father's equal touches him with a pure heart. One who doesn't understand yet that Christ is God only reaches his flesh, not his divinity. Is it so wonderful to touch his flesh when the persecutors who crucified him did this too? What is wonderful is to understand that he is the Word, God in the beginning with God, the Word through which everything was made. This is how he wanted us to know him. He said to Philip, "Have I been with you so long, and have you not known me, Philip? One who sees me sees the Father, too."

But if there is anyone who is sluggish, let him listen to John: *Children, it is the last hour.* Move! Run! Grow! For it is the last hour! This *last hour* is long, but even so it's the last one. *Hour* here means the last time, the end. It's in the last time that our Lord Jesus Christ is going to come. But some will ask, "How can it be the end? How can it be the last hour? We know that the antichrist will come first, and then the day of judgment." John was aware of these thoughts. So that people wouldn't become careless and think that it wasn't the last hour, because the antichrist was still to come, he said to them, *and as you have heard that the antichrist is to come, even now many antichrists have come to be.* Could there be many antichrists if it weren't the last hour?

Who is it he is calling the antichrists? John goes on to explain: *By this we know that it is the last hour.* By what? By the fact that *many antichrists have come to be.* You see the antichrists. *They went out from us* and so we lament the loss. But take comfort from this: *but they were not of us.* Every heretic and schismatic has gone out from us; they leave the Church. But they wouldn't go out if they were of us. Therefore before they went out they were not of us. If before they went out they weren't of us, then there are many within, many who haven't gone out but are antichrists even so. This is a bold thing to say. So why do I say it? I say it so that no one in the Church may be an antichrist. John is going to describe and point out the antichrists; now we will see them.

All of us ought to question our own consciences about whether we are antichrists. *Antichrist* means "one who is opposed to Christ." Some people have thought that *antichrist* means "one who will come before Christ, whom Christ will follow"; that the prefix is *ante,* which means "before." It isn't written that way and it doesn't mean that. *Antichrist* means "opposed to Christ."

Now who is opposed to Christ? You already know from the writer's own explanation. You understand that no one can go outside except the antichrists, that there is no possible way those who are not opposed to Christ can go outside. A person who is not opposed to Christ remains part of his body and is reckoned a member of it. Its members are never opposed to each other. The body's integrity comes from all the members together. Do you remember what the apostle Paul says of the union of members? "If one member suffers, all suffer together; if one member is honored, all rejoice together." If all members rejoice together in the honoring of one member, and if they all suffer in the suffering of one, the union of members does not admit an antichrist. Nevertheless, because at the present time Christ's body still needs healing, and because it will have perfect health only in the resurrection of the dead, there are some who exist in his body as bad substances exist in ours. When we throw these up, our bodies are relieved. In the same way, when the bad go out, the Church is relieved. When it throws up and gets rid of the bad matter, the body says, "This came out of me, but it wasn't part of me." When it says, "It wasn't part of me," it means that it wasn't cut out of its living flesh; while the bad matter was inside, it was oppressive.

They went out from us but (don't be unhappy!) *they were not of us.* How is this shown? *For if they had been of us they would surely have continued with us.* This tells you, dear friends, that many who are not of us receive the sacraments with us; they receive baptism with us. They receive with us what the faithful are aware that they receive: blessing, Eucharist, everything that is in the holy mysteries. They receive communion from the altar with us, but they are not of us! Temptation shows that they aren't of us. When temptation comes to them, it's as if they are blown away by the wind because they are chaff and not grain. They will all be blown away—I need to say this often—when the wind comes upon the Lord's threshing floor on the day of judgment. *They went out from us but they were not of us; for it they had been of us they would surely have continued with us.*

Do you want to know, my friends, how I can say with complete certainty that people who may have gone out and then returned are not antichrists, that they are not opposed to Christ? It cannot happen that those who are not antichrists should remain outside. Each person, by his own will, is either antichrist or in Christ. Either we are among his members or we are part of the bad matter. Anyone who changes for the better is a member of the body; while one who remains in his badness is bad matter. When such a one goes out, those who have been oppressed will be relieved. *They went out from us but they were not of us; for if they had been of us they would surely have continued with us; but they went out so that they might be manifest, that they were not all of us.* John added *that they might be manifest,* because even while they are within they aren't of us, but then they aren't manifest. By going out they make plain what they are.

And you have been anointed by the Holy One so that you may be manifest to yourselves. The spiritual anointing is the Holy Spirit, whose sacramental sign is the visible anointing. John says that everyone who has this anointing recognizes the bad and the good. It isn't necessary for anyone to teach them, because the anointing itself teaches them.

I am writing to you, not because you do not know the truth, but because you know it and know that no lie is of the truth. See: here we are instructed how we can recognize the antichrist. What is Christ? He is the truth. He himself said it: "I am the truth." But *no lie is of the truth,* and so everyone who lies is not yet of Christ. John didn't say that some lies are of the truth and some not. Note what he says, and don't deceive yourselves: *No lie is of the truth.*

Let us see, then, how the antichrists lie, because there is more than one kind of lie. *Who is the liar but the one who denies that Jesus is the Christ?* The name Jesus signifies one thing, and the name Christ signifies another. There is one Jesus Christ, our Savior, and Jesus is his proper name. As Moses was called by his proper name, and Elias and Abraham, so our Lord has as his proper name Jesus. Christ is the name that reveals his sacred character. We may call someone a prophet or a priest; the name Christ signifies the Anointed One, in whom is accomplished the redemption of the whole people of Israel.

The Jewish people were awaiting this Christ who was to come. Because he came in humility, they didn't recognize him. Because he was a pebble, they stumbled over him and were broken. But the pebble grew and became a great mountain. And what does Scripture tell us about it? "Whoever stumbles on that stone will be broken to pieces; and when that stone falls on anyone, it will grind him to powder." We have to distinguish between the two parts of this sentence. One who stumbles over the stone will be broken to pieces, but the one it falls on will be ground to powder. Because Christ came first in humility, people stumbled over him. Because he will be exalted when he comes in judgment, he'll grind to powder the one he falls on. But when he comes in judgment, he won't grind to powder anyone he didn't break to pieces when he first came. Anyone who didn't stumble over him when he was humble won't be afraid of him when he is exalted. You have heard it in few words, my friends: anyone who didn't stumble over him when he was humble won't be afraid of him when he is exalted. To all wicked people Christ is a stumbling stone; whatever Christ says is bitter to them.

But let us not be unhappy. *They went out from us but they were not of us; for it they had been of us they would surely have continued with us.* If they went out from us, they are antichrists. If they are antichrists, they are liars. If they are liars, they deny that Jesus is the Christ. But there is a problem that troubles both us and them: whether we are the antichrists or they are. They call us antichrists and say that we have gone out from them; we say the same thing of them. But this letter has described the antichrists. Whoever *denies that Jesus is the Christ,* that one is an antichrist. Now let us ask, then, who denies this? And let us look not at words but at actions.

Everyone who is asked replies with one voice that Jesus is the Christ. But let their voices be silent for a little while, and let us question their lives. If Scripture itself tells us that denial is possible by actions as well as words, then surely we find many antichrists who profess belief in Christ by their words but who separate themselves from him by their way of life. Do we find this in Scripture? Listen to the apostle Paul. He is talking of people of this kind when he says that "they profess to know God, but they deny him by their deeds." These are the antichrists; whoever denies Christ by his deeds is an antichrist. I don't listen to the sounds people make, but I look at the lives they lead. Actions speak. Do we need words? What evil person doesn't want to speak well? What does our Lord say to people like this? He says, in the gospel, "You hypocrites, how can you speak good when you are evil?" He is telling them, "Your voices reach my ears, but I look into your thoughts. I see ill will there, and the fruits you show me are false. I know what I must gather and where to find it. I don't gather figs from thistles or grapes from thorns. Every tree is known by its fruits." The worst liar of all is the antichrist who by his words professes that

Jesus is the Christ but denies him by his deeds. This is why he is a liar: he says one thing and does another.

And so, dear friends, if we question actions we don't just find many antichrists who have gone outside; we also find many who aren't yet manifest, who haven't begun to go out. The Church contains perjurers, deceivers, criminals, people who consult fortune tellers, adulterers, drunkards, moneylenders, dishonest merchants, and people who practice other vices I haven't time to list. These things are opposed to Christ's teaching; they are opposed to the Word of God. God's Word is Christ. Whatever is opposed to the Word of God is an antichrist, because an antichrist is one who is opposed to Christ.

Do you want to know how openly these people resist Christ? Sometimes it happens that they do something wrong, and somebody begins to reprove them. Because they don't dare to speak evil of Christ, they malign his ministers, the people who reproach them. If you show them that you are speaking Christ's words and not your own, they try as hard as they can to convince you that you are wrong, that what you say is your own and not Christ's. But if it is clear that you are speaking Christ's words, they even go against him. They begin to find fault with him. "Why," they say, "did he make us the way we are?" Don't people say this every day when they are shown to be wrong? They have been perverted by their disordered wills, so they accuse their Maker. Their Maker cries to them from heaven, the One who made us and made us new: "What did I make when I made you? I made a human being, I didn't make greed. I made a human being, I didn't make theft. I made a human being, I didn't make adultery. My works praise me."

You know this, dear friends. It's in the hymn the three boys sang that saved them from the fire. The Lord's works praise him. Heaven, earth, and sea praise him. All things in heaven praise him: angels praise him; stars praise him; all the luminaries praise him. All swimming, flying, walking, crawling things praise him. All of these things praise the Lord. Have you ever heard that greed praises the Lord? Or that drunkenness or luxury or frivolity praise him? In the hymn, whatever you didn't hear giving praise to the Lord, the Lord didn't make. Set right what you have made, so that what God made in you may be saved. But if you won't do this, if you love and embrace your sins, you are opposed to Christ. Inside or outside, you are an antichrist. Inside or outside, you are chaff. So why aren't you outside? Only because the wind hasn't reached you yet!

These things are manifest now, dear friends. No one can say, "I don't worship Christ, but I worship God, his Father." *Everyone who denies the Son has neither the Son nor the Father; and the one who confesses the Son has the Son and the Father.* John is speaking to you who are grain. As for the chaff, may they listen and become grain. Every one of you, examine your consciences. If you are a lover of the world, be changed and become a lover of Christ. Then you won't be an antichrist. And if someone should tell you that you are an antichrist, don't become angry and think you've been wronged, don't threaten to bring a charge against your accuser. Christ tells you, "Be patient—if the accusation is false, rejoice with me because I too am falsely accused by the antichrists." But if what you've heard is true, admit it in your conscience. And if you are afraid of being called an antichrist, be even more afraid of being one.

7. The Spiritual Anointing (1 John 2:24–29)

Therefore let what you heard from the beginning abide in you. If what you heard from the beginning abides in you, you too will abide in the Son and the Father. This is the promise that he has promised us. You may be thinking about recompense and saying, "See, what I've heard from the beginning I've kept safe in myself, I've complied with. I've suffered dangers, toils, temptations in order to remain faithful. What fruit does all this bring me, what recompense? What will God give me hereafter, because in this world I see myself toiling among temptations? I don't see that there is any rest here. Mortality is weighing on my soul, and my perishable body presses it down to what is beneath it. But I bear everything so that what I've heard from the beginning may abide in me, and I may say to my God, 'For the sake of the words from your mouth I have kept hard ways.' What will my recompense be?"

Listen and don't give up! If you are tending in your toil to give up, let the promised reward make you strong! What person works in a vineyard and lets the wage he's going to receive slip from his mind? If he forgets it his hands stop working. The thought of his promised recompense makes him persevere in his work. Now in that case the promise came from a human being, who can deceive you. How much more resolutely should you work on God's land when it is Truth who has made the promise? Truth can't be replaced or die or deceive the one he has promised. And what is his promise? Let us see. Is it gold, which people love here below, or silver? Is it possessions, for which people give their gold even though they love it so much? Is it delightful estates, spacious houses, hosts of servants, numerous beasts? No, it isn't for these wages that he exhorts us to persevere in our toil. What does he call our recompense? *Eternal life! This is the promise he has promised us, eternal life.*

Now you've heard me say it, and you've shouted aloud in your joy! Love what you've heard me say, and you'll find deliverance from all your troubles in the repose of eternal life. You know what it is God promises you: eternal life. You know what he threatens you with: eternal fire. What does he say to those he has placed on his right? "Come, blessed of my Father, receive the kingdom prepared for you from the foundation of the world." And what does he say to those at his left? "Go into the eternal fire which has been prepared for the devil and his angels." If you don't yet love what he has promised, at least fear what he threatens.

Remember, then, dear friends, that it is eternal life that Christ has promised us. *This,* John says, *is the promise that he has promised us, eternal life. I have written this to you about those who would deceive you.* Don't let anyone deceive you unto death. Long for the promise of eternal life. What can the world promise you? Whatever it promises, it promises to one who may die tomorrow. And how, when you leave life, will you face the One who abides forever? Will you say to him, "Someone powerful was threatening me and so I did wrong"? What did this powerful person threaten you with: was it prison, chains, fire, torture, wild beasts? Did he threaten you with eternal fire? Dread what the Almighty threatens; love what the Almighty promises. Then the whole world, whether it is promising you or threatening you, becomes contemptible.

I have written this to you about those who would deceive you; that you may know that you have an anointing and the anointing which we have received from him abides in us. There is a sacrament of anointing; the power itself is invisible. It is an invisible anointing, and this is the Holy Spirit. This invisible anointing is love. It will be for all those in whom it exists like a root that will preserve them from withering no matter how ardently the sun may burn. Everything rooted is nourished by the sun's heat, not withered by it.

And you have no need that anyone should teach you because his anointing teaches you about everything. Then what am I doing by teaching you? If *his anointing teaches you about everything,* then it seems as if there is no reason for me to work. Why should I raise my voice? I should leave you to the anointing and let it teach you. I'm asking myself and I question the apostle too (may he be patient with me). I say to John, "Did the people you were speaking to have the anointing? You said that *his anointing teaches you about everything:* why did you write this letter, then? Why were you teaching them? Why did you instruct and edify them?"

There is a great mystery here, my friends. The sound of my words strikes your ears: the Teacher is within you. Don't suppose that anyone learns anything from another human being. I can get your attention with the sound of my voice. But if there's no one within to teach you, then the sound I make accomplishes nothing. Do you want proof of this, my friends? Haven't you all heard this homily? And how many of you are going to leave here untaught? For my part, I've spoken to everyone; but those who are not spoken to from within by the anointing, who are not taught from within by the Holy Spirit, will leave untaught. Instruction that comes from without is a help, a call for attention. He who teaches hearts has his chair in heaven. That is why Jesus himself says in the gospel, "Call no one your master on earth; One alone is your Master, the Christ." Then let him speak to you from within, where no human being is present. Even if there is someone beside you, there is no one in your heart. But don't let there be "no one" in your heart. Let Christ be there! Let his anointing be in your heart, so that it doesn't thirst in the wilderness without a spring of water to refresh it. There is then an inner Master who teaches. Christ teaches; it is his inspiration that teaches. Words that sound from outside have no effect where his inspiration and anointing are lacking.

The words we speak from outside, my friends, are what a gardener is to a tree. He works from outside, he applies water and care. No matter what he may apply from without, is it he who forms the fruit? Is it he who clothes the naked branches with their shady covering of leaves? Does he do anything of this kind from without? Who does it, then? Listen to a gardener, the apostle Paul, and then you'll know what I am, and will listen to your interior Teacher: "I planted, Apollos watered, but God gave the growth. Neither the one who plants nor the one who waters is anything, but it is God who provides growth." And so this is what I say to you: whether my speaking to you is a planting or a watering, I am nothing. The one who provides growth is God; his anointing teaches you about everything.

And this anointing *is true,* John says. What he means is that the Lord's Spirit that teaches people cannot lie. This anointing *is true, and is no lie. As it has taught you, abide in it. And now, little children, abide in him, so that when he appears we may have confidence in his sight, and not be confounded by him at his coming.* You see, dear friends, we believe in Jesus, whom we haven't seen. They who saw him, who touched him, who heard the words he spoke, they have proclaimed him to us; they didn't set out on their own, but he sent them to convince the whole human race of the truth of these things. And where were they sent? You've heard the gospel: "Go, preach the good news to the whole creation under heaven." So the disciples were sent everywhere. Signs and prodigies accompanied them, so that they would be believed because they were relating what they had seen. And we believe in one we have not seen, and we await his coming. Everyone who waits for him in faith will rejoice when he comes; those who are without faith will feel shame when he comes whom they don't now see. This confusion of mind won't last a day and then pass, as happens with those who are caught in some fault and are taunted by other people. This confusion of mind will lead those who experience it to the Lord's left hand to hear him say, "Go into the eternal fire, which has been prepared for the devil and his angels."

Let us abide in his words, then, so that we won't be confounded when he comes. Christ himself says in the gospel to those who have believed in him, "If you abide in my word you are truly my disciples." And then, as if they had asked what fruit this would bring them, he went on: "And you will know the truth, and the truth will make you free." For the time being our salvation is a hope, not a reality; we don't yet possess what has been promised, but we hope for it as something to come. "He who promised is faithful." He isn't deceiving you. Only you mustn't give up, but wait for the promise. Truth cannot deceive. Don't you be a liar, professing one thing and doing another. Keep your faith; he keeps his promise. If you don't keep your faith, it's you who've cheated yourself, not he who made the promise.

If you know that he is righteous, know that everyone who does right is born of him. At present our righteousness comes from faith. There is no perfect righteousness except among the angels, and scarcely there if the angels are compared with God. And yet if there is any perfect righteousness in the souls and spirits that God has created, it is among the angels. They are holy and just and good; no fall has turned them away from God, and pride hasn't cast them down. They remain always in contemplation of the Word of God and have no delight in anything but the One who created them. In them righteousness is perfect; in us it has begun to exist—by faith, according to the Spirit.

In the psalm we sing, "Begin to make confession to the Lord!" "Begin," it says: that is, the beginning of our righteousness is our confession of sins. Have you begun not to make a defense of your sins? That's already the beginning of righteousness. Righteousness will be perfected in you when you don't want to do anything else, when death is swallowed up in victory, when you aren't tickled by wrong desires, when you no longer contend with flesh and blood, when the crown of victory and triumph over the enemy have come. At that time there will be perfect righteousness. For now we fight on. If we are fighting we are in a contest. We strike and are struck. Who'll win? We have to wait and see. But the one who wins is the one who, even when he strikes out at someone, doesn't count on his own strength but on God, who is urging him on. The devil fights against us all alone. If you are with God, you overcome the devil; but if you fight all alone, you will be beaten.

The devil is a well-practiced enemy. How many victories he wins! Consider what he has done to us: he cast our first parents out of paradise in the beginning, so that we should be born only to die. What are we to do then, because he is so skillful? Call on the Almighty against this experienced devil! There is One who can't be overcome. Let God dwell in you, and then you'll easily overcome the one who is used to winning. Who is it the devil conquers? Those in whom God doesn't dwell.

You know, my friends, that when Adam was in paradise he despised God's commandment. He raised himself up, desiring in some way to be his own master and refusing to submit to God's will. And he fell from his immortal state and his blessedness. But there was a certain man, one well trained to fight, one born subject to death; and while sitting on a dunghill eaten by worms he conquered the devil. Adam too conquered the devil—in the person of Job, because Job was of his race. And so it happened that Adam, who was overcome in paradise, overcame his enemy on a dunghill. When he was in paradise, he listened to the suggestion of the woman the devil had set against him; when he was on the dunghill, he said to Eve (in the person of his wife), "You have spoken like one of the foolish women." In paradise he listened, on the dunghill he answered; in his happiness he gave in, when he was tormented he conquered.

See what follows then, dear friends, in the letter of John. He is exhorting us to overcome the devil, certainly, but not on our own. *If you know that he is righteous,* John says, *know that everyone who does right is born of him*—born of God, of Christ. When he says *is born of him,* he is urging us on. Already, then, because we are born of him, we are perfect.

8. Living as Children of God (1 John 3:1–3)

Listen to what follows now: *See what love the Father has given us, that we should be called, and should be, children of God.* There are some who are so called, but aren't what they are called. What good does the mere name do them? How many are called physicians, and don't know how to heal? How many are called watchmen, and sleep all through the night? In the same way many are called Christians, but aren't found to be so in their actions; they aren't what they are called—not in their lives, not in their practices, their faith, their hope, or their love.

But what have you heard just now, dear friends? *See what love the Father has given us, that we should be called, and should be, children of God. The reason why the world does not know us is that it did not know him*—nor do we know the world. The whole world is Christian, and yet the whole world is godless. Throughout the whole world there are unholy people, and throughout the whole world there are holy people. And the former don't know the latter. What makes me think they don't know them? It's because they deride those who live in the right way. Consider well: perhaps even some of you are like that. If some people live a holy life and despise worldly things, or if some people have no desire to attend spectacles or to get drunk when it is the custom or—what is worse—to celebrate holy days in an unworthy way, how those who do these things laugh at those who don't! Aren't they derided if they are known? Why aren't they known? It is because *the world does not know* them. Who is the world? It's those who live in the world. I've said this often and don't want to irritate you with it. When you hear the word *world* used in a bad sense, take it to mean those who love the world; by their love they inhabit it, and because they inhabit it they deserve to bear its name.

The reason why the world does not know us is that it doesn't *know him.* He walked among us himself, the Lord Jesus Christ. He was God, in flesh, hidden in weakness. And why wasn't he known? It was because he showed people their sins. They loved the delights of sin and didn't recognize God; they loved what their fever made them want, and they wronged their physician.

What of us, then? We have already been born of him. But because we are living in hope, *Beloved,* John says, *we are God's children now.* "Now"—already? What do we have to look forward to if we are already God's children? *It does not yet appear what we shall be,* John says. But what will we be other than children of God? Listen to what follows: *We know that when he appears we shall be like him, for we shall see him as he is.* Understand this, my friends; here is something wonderful! *We know that when he appears we shall be like him, for we shall see him as he is.*

First consider what is being called *is.* You know what is called *so.* What is called *is*—and not only so called but that really *is*—is unchangeable. It always remains, it knows no change, it is in no part corruptible. It makes no progress because it is perfect, and no regress because it is eternal. And what is this? "In the beginning was the Word, and the Word was with God, and the Word was God." Again, what is this? "Who, though he was in the form of God, did not count equality with God a thing to be grasped." To see Christ in this mode of being—in the form of God, as the Word of God, the only-begotten of the Father, the Father's equal—is impossible for the wicked. But as the Word that has been made flesh, the wicked too will be able to see him. On the day of judgment the wicked will see him too, because he will come to judge in the same form as he came to be judged. In that same human form, but also as God, for "cursed be all who put their hope in man." He came as a man to be judged, and he will come as a man to judge. And if he isn't to be seen, what is this that is written: "They shall look on him whom they have pierced"?

Of the ungodly it is said that they shall see and be confounded. And why will they be confounded? He will place some at his right hand and some at his left. To those on his right he will say, "Come, blessed of my Father, receive the kingdom." To those on his left he will say, "Go into the eternal fire." The wicked will see him, but in the form of a servant; his "form of God" they won't see. Why is this? It is because they are ungodly, and the Lord himself says, "Blessed are the pure in heart, for they shall see God."

And so, my friends, we are to see a sight which no eye has seen nor ear has heard nor human heart has beheld; a sight surpassing all earthly beauties, the beauties of gold and silver, of woods and fields, of the sea and the air, of the sun and the moon and the stars, the beauty of angels, a beauty beyond all things that exist. From this beauty the beauty of all things comes.

And what will we be when we see it? What have we been promised? *We shall be like him, for we shall see him as he is.*

My tongue has done what it can, it's made the sounds of the words. The rest is for your hearts to ponder. What has John himself said in comparison with the One Who Is? What can any other human being say, so far is anyone from being his equal? Let's return to that anointing he spoke of, that anointing which teaches us from within what we cannot express. And because at the present time you can't see, your part is to desire. The whole life of a good Christian is a holy desire. You don't yet see what you desire, but desiring makes you capable of being filled when what you desire to see comes.

If you have a pocket or a sack you want to fill, and you know the immense amount of what you are to be given, you stretch whatever it is you have to fill. You know how much there is you have to put into it, and you see how small it is. By stretching it you make it capable of holding more. In the same way God stretches our desire by making us wait; he stretches our soul by making us desire; and by stretching our soul he enlarges its capacity. So let us desire, dear friends, because we are to be filled. Look at Paul stretching himself, so that he can hold what is to come: "Not that I have already obtained this, or am already perfect," he says; "brethren, I do not consider that I have made it my own." What are you doing in this life, then, if you haven't yet made it your own? "But one thing I do, forgetting what lies behind and stretching forward to what lies ahead: I press on toward the mark for the prize of the high calling of God." He describes himself as stretching forward and as pressing on toward the mark. He feels he is too little to contain what no eye has seen nor ear heard nor human heart beheld.

This is our life: to be occupied in desiring. But we are occupied in a holy desire only to the extent that we cut off our desire from the love of the world. I've already told you to empty what you want filled. You're to be filled with good, so pour out the bad. Suppose God wants to fill you up with honey. If you're full of vinegar, where will you put the honey? You must pour out what your vessel holds, and you must clean it. You must clean your vessel, working hard on it, scrubbing it, so it'll be ready for whatever is to be put in it: honey or gold or wine —whatever we say it is, that which can't be said. Whatever we want to say, it is called God. And what have we said when we've said God? Is that single syllable all we're looking for? Whatever we've had the power to say is beneath him. We must stretch out toward him, so that when he comes he'll fill us. For then *we shall be like him, for we shall see him as he is.*

And everyone who has this hope in him. . . . You see how John has established us in hope, and how Paul agrees with his fellow apostle when he says, "By hope we are saved. Now hope that is seen is not hope. For who hopes for what he sees? But if we hope for what we do not see, we wait for it with patience." Patience exercises desire. Continue, for he continues. Persevere in walking, so that you reach your goal. Your goal isn't going to move away!

And everyone who has this hope in him purifies himself as he is pure. See how he is preserving your free will when he says *puri-*

fies himself or herself. Who is it that purifies us if not God? But God doesn't purify you unless you are willing. Therefore because you join your will to God, you purify yourself. You don't purify yourself through your own resources, but through him who came to dwell within you. You have a part to play by your will, and thereby something is attributed to you. But it's only attributed to you so that you can say in the words of the psalm, "Be my helper, do not forsake me." If you say, "Be my helper," it's because you are doing something; if you weren't, how could he "help" you?

9. Avoiding Sin
(1 John 3:4–9)

Everyone who commits sin also commits wickedness. No one can say that sin is one thing and wickedness is another. Nor can anyone say, "I'm a sinner but not wicked." *Everyone who commits sin also commits wickedness; sin is wickedness.* Listen to what John says: *And you know that he appeared to take away sins, and in him there is no sin.* A sinless one came to take away sin. If there had been sin in him, it would have had to be taken away from him too; he himself wouldn't have been able to take it away. *No one who abides in him sins.* Insofar as anyone abides in him, so far that one doesn't sin. *No one who sins has either seen him or known him.*

There is a problem here. *No one who sins has either seen him or known him.* This isn't surprising. We haven't seen him but we will see him someday; we haven't known him but we will know him. We believe in One whom we haven't known. Or is it that we have known him "by faith" but not yet "by sight"? Yes, in faith we both see him and know him. If faith doesn't yet see him, why are we called "the enlightened ones"? There is enlightenment that comes from faith, and there is enlightenment that comes from sight. Now, while we are pilgrims, "we walk by faith, not by sight." Our righteousness also, then, comes from faith, not from sight, and it will be complete only when we shall see "by sight." In the meantime, let us not forsake the righteousness that comes from faith, because "the righteous man lives by faith," as the Apostle says. *No one who abides in him sins,* for *no one who sins has either seen him or known him.* No one who sins believes, but those who believe, insofar as it depends on their faith, don't sin.

Little children, let no one deceive you. One who does right is righteous as he also is righteous. Should we, when we hear that we are *righteous as he also is righteous,* think that we are God's equals? You have to understand what that *as* means. A little while back John said that *everyone purifies himself as he is pure.* Is our purity already equal to and identical with God's purity, and our righteousness equal to and identical with God's righteousness? Who would say this? The word *as* isn't always used to express identicalness. For example, if someone looks at this great church and wants to build one that is smaller but of the same proportions—say the length being double the width— anyone could look at it and say that it is *as* this one is. But this one is, shall we say, one hundred cubits in length and that one thirty. Thus, one is *as* the other is, but also unequal to it. You can see that *as* doesn't always express equality and identicalness. Another example: consider how different are a person's face and its image in a mirror. There is one face in the image and one in the body. The image exists as a likeness, and the body as a reality. And what do we say? There are eyes here *as* there are there; ears here *as* there. The realities are different, but *as* expresses a resemblance.

One who commits sin is of the devil; for the devil sins from the beginning. Do you know what John means when he says *is of the devil?* He means that someone is of the devil by imitation. The devil didn't make anyone or beget anyone or create anyone. But whoever imitates the devil is, so to speak, born of him. He becomes a child of the devil by imitating him, not by being literally born of him. How is it that you are a child of Abraham? Did Abraham beget you? Or is it the way that the Jews became children of the devil? They were Abraham's children, born of his flesh, but they didn't imitate his faith. If those who were born of Abraham were disinherited because they didn't imitate him, you, who weren't born of him, become his child by imitating him. But if you imitate the devil, who was proud and undutiful and against God, you will be his child—not because he created or begot you but by imitation.

For this purpose the Son of God appeared. Indeed, dear friends, all sinners are born of the devil, inasmuch as they are sinners.

Adam was made by God, but when he consented to the devil he was born of the devil, and all his descendants are like him. We were born of this condemnation. If we are born sinless, why do we run with our infants to baptism for their absolution? Dear friends, consider these two births, Adam's and Christ's: both are human; but one of them is only a man, the other a man who is God. Through the man who is God we are made righteous. One birth has cast us down to death; the other has raised us up to life. One drags sin along with it; the other sets us free from sin. Christ came as man for this reason: to destroy people's sins. *For this purpose the Son of God appeared: to destroy the works of the devil.*

There is a problem that I am trying to solve. We call ourselves sinners. Anyone who claims to be sinless is a liar. You must remember what came earlier in this letter of John's: "If we say we have no sin we deceive ourselves and the truth is not in us." Yet in the present passage you are told that *no one who is born of God sins. . . . No one who sins has either seen him or known him. . . . Everyone who commits sin is of the devil.* Sin is not from God. John alarms us here! What are we to do, caught as we are between these two texts from the same letter? If we confess that we are sinners, we're afraid we'll be told we are not born of God. But if we call ourselves righteous and say that we are without sin, John's words strike us from the other side.

I'm keeping this difficulty before you, so that your exertion may be a prayer on behalf of us all and may lead God to free us and give us a way out. Otherwise, someone may find in John's word an occasion for falling away—the word that was preached and written down only for healing and salvation.

John says, *No one who is born of God commits sin for his seed abides in him; and he cannot sin because he is born of God.* He's bound us tightly. But perhaps this will help. Has he said "cannot sin" with reference to one particular sin rather than to every sin? Accordingly, when he says that *no one who is born of God commits sin,* you should understand a certain sin which no one born of God can commit. That sin is one which, if anyone commits it, confirms all the others; but if it isn't committed the others are destroyed. What sin is it? To act against the commandment. What commandment? "A new commandment I give to you, that you love one another." Note this well. This commandment of Christ's is called love; through this love sins are destroyed. If this commandment isn't kept, the sin of not keeping it is grave and is the root of all sins.

Consider this, my friends. I've proposed something that solves our problem. There is a sin that can't be committed by one who is born of God, and this sin is to act contrary to Christ's commandment, contrary to the new covenant: "A new commandment I give to you, that you love one another." No one who acts contrary to charity and neighborly love should dare to boast and claim to be born of God. There are certain sins that those who do love their neighbor cannot commit, and the chief of these is hatred of a sister or brother. And what of the other sins of which John says that "if we say we have no sin we deceive ourselves and the truth is not in us"? Let us take confidence from another passage of Scripture: "Love buries a multitude of sins." It's love, then, that I am commending to you, and love that this letter commends.

And this is perfect love: to be ready to die for your sister or brother. The Lord showed us an example of this in himself. He died for all people, and as he died he prayed for those who were crucifying him, saying, "Father, forgive them, for they know not what they do." But if he was the only one who did it, then he wasn't a teacher because he had no disciples. But there were disciples who came after him and did the same thing. As Stephen was being stoned, he knelt and said, "Lord, do not hold this sin against them." He loved the people who were killing him, because he was dying for them too. And listen to the apostle Paul: "I myself," he said, "will be spent for your souls." Paul was among those for whom Stephen sought forgiveness when he was dying at their hands.

So this is perfect love. If someone's love is so great that he or she is ready even to die for a sister or brother, then in that person love is perfect. But is it ever perfect when it is born? No, it is born in order that it may be made perfect. When it has been born, it is nourished; when it is nourished, it is strengthened; when it has been strengthened, it becomes perfect. And when it has reached perfection what does it say? "To me to live is Christ and to die is gain. My desire is to depart and to be with Christ, for that is by far the best thing; but to remain in the flesh is necessary for your sakes." Paul was willing to live for their sakes, for whom he was willing to die. And this, as I've said, dear friends, is perfect love. A person who is born of God possesses it. Pay attention now, my friends, and see what I am saying.

A baptized person has received the sacrament of birth. That person has the sacrament, a sacrament that is great, divine, holy, and ineffable. Consider how great it is: it makes a new person by the remission of all sins! But those who are made new should look into the heart to see whether what was done in the body has been brought to perfection in the heart. Let them see whether they possess love, and then let them say, "I am born of God." Those who don't have love do indeed have the brand or mark which was set on them, but they are only wandering deserters. Let them have love! Otherwise they shouldn't claim to be born of God. But, someone may say, "I have the sacrament." Listen to what the Apostle says: "If I know all mysteries"—this means sacraments—"and I have all faith so as to move mountains, but have not love, I am nothing."

10. The Law of Love
(1 John 3:10–18)

My friends, this is what I said to you, if you remember, when I began to read this letter: there is nothing in it so recommended to us as love. Even if John seems to talk of various other things, he always comes back to love. He wants whatever he says brought to bear on love. Let us see if he does that here.

No one who is born of God commits sin. We are asking what sin he means, because if you understand him to mean all sin this is contrary to that other text: "If we say we have no sin we deceive ourselves and the truth is not in us." So let him tell us what sin he means, let him instruct us. It may be that I spoke rashly when I said that the sin meant here is the transgression of love. I said this because he said earlier that "one who hates his brother is in the darkness and walks in the darkness and does not know where he is going because the darkness has blinded his eyes." Has he said something more specific in this later part and spoken of love by name? See how this sentence ends: *No one who is born of God commits sin for his seed abides in him.* God's "seed" is his word, as the Apostle says: "For I have begotten you through the gospel." *And he cannot sin because he is born of God.* Let John tell us in what we cannot sin. *In this are manifested the children of God and the children of the devil. Everyone who is not righteous is not of God, nor one who does not love his brother.*

One who does not love his brother or sister: this phrase makes everything clear. Love alone distinguishes the children of God from those of the devil. They can all sign themselves with the sign of Christ's cross; they can all respond Amen and sing Alleluia; they may all be baptized and come to church; and they may build churches; but the children of God are distinguished from the children of the devil only by love. Those who love are born of God, those who don't are not. This is the great sign, the great difference. Possess whatever you will, but if you lack this, the rest does you no good. Have nothing else; only possess this and you've fulfilled the law. "One who loves another has fulfilled the law," says the Apostle; and "Love is the fullness of the law."

I take this to be the pearl the man in the gospel was seeking. When he found this single pearl, "He sold all that he had and bought it." Love is this "pearl of great value." Without it, nothing you have does you any good. If you have it alone, it is enough for you. Now your vision is "by faith," later it will be "by sight." If we love now when we don't see, how we shall embrace love when we do see! But how are we trained in this love? In love of our neighbor. You can tell me you haven't seen God. Can you tell me you haven't seen your brother or your sister? Love them! If you love the brother and the sister you see, at the same time you'll see God too, because you'll be seeing love itself, and within love God dwells.

Everyone who is not righteous is not of God, nor one who does not love his brother. For this is the message. See how he confirms it: *This is the message we have heard from the beginning, that we should love one another.* He's shown us where this message comes from. Anyone who acts contrary to this commandment commits that accursed sin into which those not born of God fall.

Not like Cain who was of the evil one and murdered his brother. And why did he murder him? Because his own deeds were evil and his brother's righteous. Where there is envy there can't be any love of sister or brother. Dear friends, pay attention to this. Envy is incompatible with love. It's the devil's sin that is in the envious person, because it was by envy that the devil cast a human down. The devil fell and he envied the one who was still standing. It wasn't in order to stand himself that he wanted to cast the human down, but so that he wouldn't be alone in his fall.

Keep firmly in your minds from this example that there can be no envy in love. You have it clearly stated when Paul is praising love: "Love is not jealous." There was no love in Cain. And if there hadn't been love in Abel, God wouldn't have accepted his sacrifice. When both brought their offerings—one from the fruits of the earth and the other from the young of his flock—you aren't to think, my friends, that God despised one and prized the other. God wasn't watching their hands; rather he was looking into their hearts. He had regard for the sacrifice of the one he saw coming with love; he turned his eyes away from the sacrifice of the one who brought his offering with envy. What John calls Abel's good deeds, then, is love; and what he calls Cain's evil deeds is his hatred of his brother. And it wasn't enough for him to hate his brother, he even envied his good deeds. Because Cain wouldn't imitate Abel, he desired to kill him. From this it is clear that he was a child of the devil, and that Abel was one of God's righteous ones. In this way can people be distinguished, my friends. Don't pay attention to their words but to their deeds and their hearts. Those who don't do good for their sisters and brothers show what is in them. People are tested by temptations.

Do not wonder, brethren, if the world hates us. Do I have to keep telling you what "the world" is? It's not heaven or earth or any other of God's works. It's those who love the world. Some of you find it tedious that I say this so often, but I have a reason: There are some who can't answer if you ask them whether I've said it! Therefore, if I hammer it in, perhaps something may stick. What is the world? Taken in a good sense, it is heaven and earth and God's works in them. In this sense it is said that "the world was made through him." Still in the good sense, the world is the entire earth, as these words of John show: "He is the expiation for our sins, and not for ours only but also for those of the whole world." *The world* in the good sense means "all the faithful scattered over the earth." But *the world* in the bad sense means "lovers of the world." Those who love the world cannot love their sisters and brothers.

If the world hates us, we know. . . . What is it we know? *That we have passed from death to life.* How do we know it? *Because we love the brethren.* Don't question anyone else. Turn to your own heart. If you find love of your sisters and brothers there, you can be sure you've passed from death to life. Already you are at Christ's right hand. Don't be concerned that your glory is hidden now. When the Lord comes, then will you appear in glory! Even now you're full of life, but it's still winter. Your root is alive even though your branches seem to be dead. Your pith, which is full of vigor, is inside; your leaves and fruit are inside. They are waiting for summer. And so *we know that we have passed from death to life because we love the brethren. One who doesn't love abides in death.*

Dear friends, don't think that it's a small matter to hate and not to love. Listen to what follows: *Everyone who hates his brother is a murderer.* Now if any one of you takes hatred of your brother or sister lightly, will you also take lightly the murder you commit in your heart? You aren't lifting your hand to kill anyone, yet God already counts you a murderer. The person you hate is still alive, but you are already judged a killer. *Everyone who hates his brother is a murderer, and you know that no murderer has eternal life abiding in him.*

By this we know love. John is speaking of love's perfection, the perfection I've already put before you. *By this we know love, that he laid down his life for us; and we ought to lay down our lives for the brethren.* How does love begin, my friends? Keep listening. You've heard what its perfection is. The Lord has put its end and measure before us in the gospel: "Greater love no one has," he says, "than that he lay down his life for his friends." It's the perfection of love that he shows us in the gospel and commends to us here. But you question yourselves: "When can we have such love?" Don't despair of yourselves too quickly! Perhaps it's been born but isn't perfect yet. Cherish it so that it isn't stifled. "But," you'll say to me, "how am I to know? We know how love is perfected; let us hear how it begins."

John goes on to tell you. *If anyone has the world's goods and sees his brother suffering hunger and closes his heart against him, how can the love of God abide in him?* See where love begins. If you're not yet capable of dying for your sister or brother, be capable even now of giving him some of your goods. Let love stir your heart to action now, not to do what you do for display, but out of an inner richness of compassion, thinking only of your fellow human being who is in need. If you can't give what you have to spare to your sister or brother, are you able to lay down your life for anyone?

Say you have money in your pocket, which thieves can take away from you. Even if they don't, you'll leave it when you die, provided it doesn't leave you while you are still alive. What are you going to do with it? Your sister or brother is hungry and in need—anxious, maybe, pressed by some creditor. Your sister or brother has nothing, but you possess something. This person is a sister or a brother. Together you were purchased. One price was paid for you both. You were both redeemed by the blood of Christ. See if you have compassion, you who have *the world's goods.* Perhaps you ask, "What does this have to do with me? Am I to give my money, so that this person won't be inconvenienced?" If this is what your heart answers you, the love of the Father is not abiding in you. If the love of the Father doesn't abide in you, you aren't born of God. How can you boast of being a Christian? You have the name and not the deeds. But if your work conforms to the name, let anyone who wants call you a pagan. Prove yourself a Christian by your deeds. If your deeds don't prove it, everyone can call you Christian, but what good does the name do you when the reality is lacking? *If anyone has the world's goods and sees his brother in need and closes his heart against him, how can the love of God abide in him?* And then John goes on: *Little children, let us not love in word only and speech, but in deed and in truth.*

I think it must be plain to you now, my friends, how great and necessary is this secret and mysterious reality. All Scripture tells you of the value of love, but I don't think it is set forth anywhere more fully than in this letter. I pray and beseech you in the Lord's name to remember these things you have heard and to come eagerly and listen intently to what I have still to say before we finish this letter. Open your hearts to the good seed. Root out the thorns, so that what is being sown in you won't be choked but that the harvest may increase. Let the farmer rejoice and get his barn ready for you, the grain—and not prepare his fire for you, the chaff.

11. True Love
(1 John 3:18–21)

If you remember, my friends, yesterday I ended my homily at this sentence, which should still be in your hearts, since it was the last you heard: *Little children, let us not love in word only and speech, but in deed and in truth.* The question is, in what deed or in what truth do we recognize one who loves God or loves a sister or brother? John told us earlier at what point love becomes perfect; it is what the Lord too told us in the gospel: "Greater love no one has than this, that he lay down his life for his friends." John said, "As he laid down his life for us, we too should lay down our lives for the brethren." This is the perfection of love; it's not possible to find any greater.

But love isn't perfect in everyone. No one in whom it is imperfect should despair if what can be perfected has already been born. Of course, if it's born it has to be cherished and brought by the right kind of nourishment to its proper perfection. We asked where this rudimentary love begins, and we found the answer immediately: "If anyone has the world's goods and sees his brother in need and closes his heart against him, how can the love of God abide in him?" This is where love begins, dear friends: to give of what you have to spare to one who is in need, to one in some difficulty; it is to give of your temporal abundance to free a sister or brother from temporal distress. This is where love starts. When it's begun in this way, if you nourish it with God's word and with the hope of a future life, you'll come at last to the perfection of love. Then you will be ready to lay down your life for your sisters and brothers.

But because many deeds of this kind are done by people with some other intention in mind, by people who don't love their sisters and brothers, let us ask again: what deed, what love does he mean? Can there by any plainer deed than giving to the poor? Yet many do it for display, not out of love. Can there be any greater deed than dying for others? Many want to be thought to do this; yet they do it out of vainglory, to get a name, not out of love that comes from their depths.

It remains that those people truly love their sister or brother who reassure themselves, in their hearts before God, where he alone sees, and question in their hearts whether they truly do what they do for love of their sisters and brothers. And that eye which penetrates their hearts, where no human being can reach, is their witness. So Paul the apostle, because he was ready to die for his brethren, said, "I will myself be spent for your souls." But because God saw this in his heart, and the people he was addressing did not, Paul told them, "For me it is a very small thing to be judged by you or by any human day," meaning tribunal. And he shows us in another place that these things are often done out of empty display, not on the solid ground of love. When he was speaking the praises of love he said, "If I give away all I have to the poor and if I deliver my body to be burned, but have not love, I gain nothing." Can anyone do this without love? We must answer yes. There are people who have no love who brought division to our unity. Look at them and you will see many who give large amounts to the poor. You'll see them ready to undergo death, to the point that if they don't find a persecutor they destroy themselves. There is no doubt that they do this without love.

So let us withdraw into our consciences. The Apostle says, "For our boast is this, the testimony of our conscience." Let us withdraw into our consciences. The same Apostle says, "But let each one test his own work, and then his reason to boast will be in himself alone and not in another." Let each of us test his or her own work, whether it springs from the vein of love, whether the branches of good deeds come from the root of love. "But let each one test his own work," Paul says, "and then his reason to boast will be in himself alone and not in another": not when someone else bears witness to you but when your own conscience does it.

This then is what John is teaching us here. *By this we know that we are of the truth,* when we love in deed and in truth, not just in word and speech, *and we reassure our hearts before him.* What does *before him* mean? It means there, where God sees us. This is why the Lord himself says in the gospel, "Beware of practicing your righteousness before men in order to be seen by them; otherwise, you will have no reward from your Father who is in heaven." And what does "do not let your left hand know what your right hand is doing" mean if the "right hand" isn't a pure conscience and the "left hand" isn't worldly desire? Many people perform marvels through worldly desire. That's the left hand working, not the right. It's the right hand that must work while the left hand remains ignorant. Then no worldly desire is mixed in when we do something good out of love. But how can we be sure of this? You are before God. Question your heart, look at what you've done and what you were seeking when you did it. Was it your salvation? Or was it empty human praise? Look within yourself, for nobody can judge someone he doesn't see.

If we reassure our hearts, let it be *before him. For if our hearts condemn us*—if they accuse us from within, because we don't act with the intention we ought to have—*God is greater than our hearts, and he knows everything.* You hide your heart from other human beings. Hide it from God if you can! There was a sinner once who was afraid and confessed to him, "Where shall I go from your spirit? And where shall I flee from your face?" He was looking for a way to escape God's judgment, and he didn't find any. Where is God absent? "If I ascend into heaven you are there," he says; "if I descend into hell you are present." Where will you go? Where will you flee? Do you want some advice? If what you want is to flee from him, flee toward him. Flee toward him by confessing to him, not by hiding from him. Hide from him you can't, but you can confess to him. Tell him,

"You are my refuge," and let love be nourished in you, because only love leads you to life. Let your conscience bear witness to you that it is of God. If it's of God, don't desire to display it before people, because their praise isn't going to raise you up to heaven or their censure cast you down. Let him behold you, who gives you the crown. Let him be the witness, who is the judge by whom you'll receive it. *God is greater than our hearts, and he knows everything.*

Beloved, if our hearts do not condemn us, we have confidence before God. What does it mean to say, *if our hearts do not condemn us?* If our hearts respond to us in truth that we love, that the love in us is genuine, that it's sincere, not feigned, that it seeks the salvation of others, not expecting any profit from them beyond their salvation, then *we have confidence before God; and we will receive from him whatever we ask because we keep his commandments.* Our confidence isn't in the sight of other people, then, but where God himself sees, in our hearts. *And we will receive from him whatever we ask,* but only *because we keep his commandments.* What are his commandments? Do I have to be continually repeating it? "A new commandment I give to you, that you love one another." It's love he's talking about, love he's commending to us. Whoever has love of sisters and brothers, and has it before God, where God sees, and whoever's heart when it is honestly questioned makes no other response than that it contains a genuine root of love for good fruits to come from, this person has confidence before God. And whatever such persons ask they will receive from Him, because they keep his commandments.

12. Unanswered Prayer
(1 John 3:22)

Here a question comes up. If any particular person, if you or I, asks anything from the Lord our God and doesn't receive it, anyone can always say, "He has no love." We can easily say this of any person of our own time. Anyone can think what he wills of another. A more serious question comes up concerning those persons who we are certain wrote as saints and are now with God. If you consider John's words, it all seems clear. If you take examples into account, it becomes obscure. Nothing could be clearer than his words: *We will receive from him whatever we ask because we keep his commandments and do those things that are pleasing in his sight.* If we pray, John says, and if our hearts don't accuse us but declare in God's sight that we have true love in us, *we will receive from him whatever we ask.*

I've already told you, my friends, not to look to me. What am I? What are you? What are we but the Church of God, which is known to everyone? If God please we belong to his Church, we abide in it by love. Let us persevere in it if we want to manifest the love we have.

But consider the apostle Paul. What evil are we to think of him? Did he not love his sisters and brothers? Did he not have the testimony of his conscience in God's sight? Did he lack that root of love from which all good fruits proceed? Who would be foolish enough to say this? Where then have we found that the Apostle asked and didn't receive? He himself says, "Lest I be exalted by the greatness of the revelations, a thorn was given to me in my flesh, an angel of Satan to harass me. Three times I besought the Lord about this, that he would take it from me; and he said to me: 'My grace is sufficient for you, for strength is made perfect in weakness.'" You see, his prayer that the angel of Satan be taken from him wasn't heard. Why wasn't it? Because it wasn't for his good. His prayer was heard for his good, not according to his desire. This is a great mystery, my friends; I want you to recognize it and never lose sight of it in your temptations. The saints are heard for their good in all things. They are always heard for their eternal good. This is what they desire; in what concerns this, their prayers are always heard.

We have to distinguish God's different ways of hearing. We find some people who aren't granted what they want, but what is for their good. And we find others who are granted what they want, but it is not for their good. Don't lose sight of this distinction. Keep in mind the example of Paul, who was not heard according to his will but for his good: "My grace is sufficient for you," God told him, "for strength is made perfect in weakness." "You asked me, you cried out to me, three times you cried out to me, and I heard what you cried to me. I didn't turn away my ears from you. I know what I have to do. You want to escape the medicine that stings you, yet I know the weakness that oppresses you." This was a man heard for his good, but not given what he wanted.

Where do we find people given what they want but not for their good? Do we think we can find some wicked, ungodly person treated in this way? If I put some such person before you, you can always say to me, "It's you who call him wicked; he was righteous. If he hadn't been, God wouldn't have heard him." But the example I'm going to give you is someone whose wickedness and ungodliness you can't doubt: it's the devil himself. He asked to have a holy man, Job, to tempt, and he received what he asked for. The Apostle asked that the thorn in his flesh be removed, and it wasn't. But it was still Paul rather than the devil whom God heard. The Apostle was heard for his good, though he wasn't given what he wanted. The devil was given what he wanted, but for his damnation. Job was given over to the devil to be tempted, so that his constancy might be a torment for his tempter.

So we have to understand that although God doesn't give us what we want, he gives what we need for our salvation. What if you ask your doctor for something harmful, something he knows is harmful? Suppose you ask for a drink of cold water. You can't say he doesn't hear you when he gives it to you right away, if it's for your good. But if it's not good for you, he doesn't give it. If he contradicts your will, does that mean he hasn't heard you? Or has he heard you and done what is good for your health?

Have love in yourselves, dear friends. Have love and be at peace. Even when you aren't given what you ask for, you are heard, only you aren't aware of it. Many people have been given into their own hands to their harm. The Apostle says of them that "God gave them up to the desires of their own hearts." One such person asked for great riches. While he was poor he had little to fear. When he began to grow rich, he became the prey of someone more powerful. Wasn't he heard to his harm? He wanted to possess what would attract robbers to him; no one sought him while he was poor.

Learn to make your needs known to God, entrusting yourself to your Physician to do what he judges best. Confess your illness and let him apply the remedy. It's for you to hold fast to love. He's going to cut you and sting you. If you cry out and he doesn't listen while he is cutting and stinging and making you suffer, it's because he knows how far the disease reaches. You want him to take his hands off you, yet he knows how deep the wound is and how far he has to go. He's not listening to what you want, but granting what will bring you good health.

You may be sure, my friends, that what the Apostle says is true: "We do not know how to pray as we ought, but the Spirit himself intercedes for us with sighs too deep for words . . . for he is interceding for the saints." What does "the Spirit himself intercedes for the saints" signify, if not that love is brought about in you through the Spirit? And so the same Apostle says that "God's love has been poured out in our hearts through the Holy Spirit, which has been given to us." Love itself sighs, love itself prays. The one who gives it can't close his ears against it. Be at peace. Let love ask and God's ears are there to hear. He doesn't do what you want, but he does what is expedient for you. Therefore, John says, *We will receive from him whatever we ask.* As I've said, if you understand "for your good" there's no problem here. If you don't, you have a problem, a serious one that makes you a defamer of the apostle Paul. *We will receive from him whatever we ask because we keep his commandments and do those things that are pleasing in his sight;* within, where he sees us.

13. Faith and Love
(1 John 3:23–4:3)

What are God's commandments? *This,* John says, *is his commandment, that we should believe in the name of his Son Jesus Christ and love one another.* You see what his commandment is, and you understand that anyone who acts contrary to this commandment commits the sin from which everyone born of God is free. You know that all we are asked to do is love one another. *One who keeps his commandment will abide in him, and he in that one. And by this we know that he abides in us, by the Spirit which he has given us.* Isn't it evident that what the Holy Spirit does in us is cause us to have love and charity? Isn't what the apostle Paul says true: "God's love has been poured out in our hearts through the Holy Spirit which has been given to us"? John has been speaking of love and saying that we must examine our hearts in God's sight. "If our hearts do not condemn us"—in other words, if our hearts confess that any good work is done out of love for our sister and brother—then comes our present passage, *This is his commandment,* and so on. If you find that you have love, then you have the Spirit of God to give you understanding—something truly necessary.

In the earliest times the Holy Spirit would fall upon believers, and they would speak in languages they hadn't learned, as the Spirit gave them utterance. This was a sign suited to the time. It was fitting that the Holy Spirit be signified by all languages, because the gospel of God was going to spread over the whole earth by means of those languages. The sign was given and then passed away. Do we still expect the people we lay hands on, so that they may receive the Holy Spirit, to speak in tongues? When we laid our hands on the neophytes last Easter, did each of you watch to see whether they'd speak in tongues? And when you saw that they didn't, was any one of you so wrongheaded as to say that they hadn't received the Holy Spirit?

If the presence of the Holy Spirit isn't made known by the testimony of these miracles in our day, how is it now done? How do we recognize that we have received the Holy Spirit? Let us ask our hearts. If we love our sisters and brothers, the Spirit of God abides in us. Let us look, let us examine ourselves before the eyes of God. Let us see if we have in us a love of peace and unity, a love of the Church spread throughout the world. Don't take note only whether you love the sister or brother who is right in front of you. We have many sisters and brothers we don't see, and we are linked to them as well in the unity of the Spirit. Is it so strange that they aren't with us? We are all of us members of a single body, we have a single Head in heaven. My friends, no one's right eye can observe the left, and vice versa. You might say our eyes don't know each other. But can we say that they don't know each other in the love that holds our body together?

Let me show you that in the bond of love they do know each other. When both eyes are open, the right eye can't focus on something without the left one focusing on it too. Direct your right eye toward some object without the other if you can! They converge and they move together. They have one aim even though they are in different places. Accordingly, if all those who love God with you have one aim with you, don't consider that your bodies are in different places. You have the eyes of your hearts fixed together on the light of truth.

So then, if you want to know that you've received the Spirit, question your hearts. You may have the sacrament without having its power. Question your hearts! If there is love of your sisters and brothers there, be at peace. There can't be any love without the Spirit of God, for Paul calls out to you, "God's love has been poured out in our hearts through the Holy Spirit which has been given to us."

Beloved, do not believe every spirit, but test the spirits to see whether they are of God. In the gospel the Holy Spirit was called water when the Lord cried out and said, "If anyone thirst, let him come to me and drink. He who believes in me, out of his heart shall flow rivers of living water." The Evangelist himself tells us what the Lord meant. "Now this," he says, "he said of the Spirit which those who were to believe in him would receive." Why was it the Lord didn't baptize many people? What does John tell us about this? "For the Spirit had not yet been given because Jesus had not yet been glorified." They had received a baptism, then, but they hadn't yet received the Holy Spirit, which the Lord sent from heaven on the day of Pentecost. The Lord had to be glorified before the Spirit could be given. But before he was glorified and sent the Spirit, he was calling people to prepare themselves to receive the water, about which he said, "If anyone thirst, let him come to me and drink" and "He who believes in me, out of his heart shall flow rivers of living water."

What are these rivers of living water? What is this water? Don't question me, question the gospel. "Now this," it says, "he said of the Spirit which those who were to believe in him would receive." The water of the sacrament is one thing, then, and the water which signifies the Spirit of God is another. The water of the sacrament is visible, and the water of the Spirit is not. The former washes the body and signifies what happens in the soul, but it is by the Spirit of God, which no heretics, none who cut themselves off from the Church, can have. Neither do they possess the Spirit who don't openly separate themselves, but who are cut off by their wrongdoing. These are not grain, but are ones whirled around inside the Church like chaff on the threshing floor.

We've read in this letter, *Do not believe every spirit.* This is confirmed by the words of Solomon: "Keep far from strange water." What does *water* mean? Here it means "Spirit." Does it always mean this? No, not always. In certain places it means "Spirit"; in others "baptism"; in the book of Revelation it means "peoples or nations"; in another place it means "counsel." Thus you find it said, "Counsel is a fountain of life for those who possess it." Therefore, in various places in Scripture, *water* means various things. But here you've heard the Holy Spirit called water, and this is not my interpretation but the testimony of the gospel: "This he said of the Spirit which those who were to believe in him would receive." If, then, the Holy Spirit is meant by *water,* and this letter tells us not to *believe every spirit, but to test the spirits to see whether they are of God,* we should understand that for this reason Solomon told us to "keep far from strange water, and from a strange fountain do not drink." What does this last phrase mean? Do not believe a strange spirit.

We still have to find out how the Spirit of God is tested. John has given us a sign, one we may find difficult. But let us see. *Test the spirits to see whether they are of God; for many false prophets have gone out into the world.* There you have indicated all the heretics and schismatics. How am I to test the spirits, then? John goes on: *By this is known the Spirit of God.* Prick up the ears of your hearts! We were troubled and asking, "Who knows, who discerns?" See, he is about to give us a sign. *By this is known the Spirit of God; every spirit which confesses that Jesus Christ has come in the flesh is of God, and every spirit which does not confess that Jesus Christ has come in the flesh is not of God. This is the antichrist, of which you heard that it was coming, and now it is in the world.*

We've pricked up our ears, so to speak, in order to discern the spirits. And what we've heard doesn't seem to help at all. *Every spirit which confesses that Jesus Christ has come in the flesh is of God.* But is the spirit we find in heretics *of God,* then, because they confess that Jesus Christ has come in the flesh? Do all heresies have the Spirit of God? Are they not false prophets, then? Surely they are antichrists: "They went out from us, but they were not of us." You have already heard us say that the one who denies that Jesus Christ came in the flesh is an antichrist. That's when we asked who it is who *denies that Jesus is the Christ,* because none will say they deny this. And we found that there are some who deny it by their deeds, and we brought testimony from the Apostle, who said that "they profess to know God, but they deny him by their deeds." So then, let us now again look at deeds, not at words.

Which is the spirit that is not of God? It's the one that denies that Jesus came in the flesh. Which is the one that confesses that Jesus came in the flesh? Here, my friends, is where we have to look at the works and not stop at the sounds people make. Let us ask *why* Christ came in the flesh, and then we'll find those who deny it. If you pay attention to words, you'll hear many heretics confessing it. But truth convicts them. Why did Christ come in the flesh? Wasn't he God? Wasn't it written of him, "In the beginning was the Word, and the Word was with God, and the Word was God"? Isn't it he who fed the angels, and does it still? Didn't he come here to us without leaving heaven? Didn't he ascend without forsaking us? Then why did he come in the flesh? It's because he needed to put before us the hope of resurrection. He was God but he came in the flesh. Death is not possible for God, but for flesh it is. He came in the flesh, then, so that he could die for us. But why did he come to die for us? "Greater love than this no one has, that he lay down his life for his friends." It was love, therefore, that led him to become flesh. And so whoever does not have love denies that Christ came in the flesh.

Now, question all the heretics: Did Christ come in the flesh?—He did. This is what I believe and profess.—No, you deny it!—How do I deny it? Didn't you hear me say it!—No, I convict you of denying it. You say it with your voice, but deny it in your heart. You say it in words, but you deny it in your deeds. How, you ask me, do I deny it in my deeds? I answer: Because Christ came in the flesh, he was able to die for us. He died for us because in that way he taught us great love. "Greater love than this no one has, that he lay down his life for his friends." You do not have love, because for the sake of your own reputation you break unity.

Understand from this which spirit is of God. Strike these earthen vessels and see if they crack and give a dull sound; or see if they ring loud and clear, see if love is there. You withdraw from the unity of the whole world. You divide the Church by schisms, you rend Christ's body. He came in the flesh to gather people together; you make your outcry to disperse them. The Spirit of God is the one that says that Jesus came in the flesh, that says it by deeds not by words, by loving not by sounding off. That is not the Spirit of God which denies that Jesus Christ came in the flesh.

It denies here too, not by mouth but by life, not by words but by deeds. It is clear, then, how we may recognize our sisters and brothers. Many people seem to be inside the Church but aren't really; but no one is outside who isn't really so.

14. God Is Love
(1 John 4:4–8)

Now, little children, John says, *you are of God, and have overcome him.* Who is "him"? Whom but the antichrist? John has already said that everyone who does away with Jesus Christ and denies that he came in the flesh is not of God. We explained, if you remember, that all those who transgress love deny that Jesus came in the flesh. Jesus had no need to come, except for the sake of love. The love enjoined on us here is the same that Jesus himself enjoins in the gospel: "Greater love than this no one can have, that he lay down his life for his friends." How would God's Son have been able to lay down his life for us, unless he clothed himself in flesh in which he could die? Therefore all those who transgress love, no matter what they may say, deny by their lives that Christ came in the flesh. They are antichrists, wherever they are, wherever they've entered.

And what is John telling those who are citizens of the homeland we are longing for? He tells them, *You have overcome him.* And how have they done it? *Because greater is he who is in you than he who is in this world.* John doesn't want them to attribute their victory to their own powers, and thereby be overcome by the presumption of pride. Anyone the devil makes proud he overcomes. John wants them to remain humble. He has told them, *You have overcome him,* and everyone who hears the word *overcome* will lift up their heads and expect to be praised. But don't extol yourselves. See who it is in you who has overcome. You have overcome *because greater is he who is in you than he who is in this world.* Be humble. Bear your Lord. Be the beast he rides. It is good for you that he guides and leads. If you haven't him as your rider, you may lift your necks, you may strike out with your heels, but it's your loss, because this liberty sends you to the wild beasts to be devoured.

They are of the world, therefore they speak the language of the world, and the world listens to them. Who are they who speak the language of the world? It is those who speak against love. You've heard the Lord when he said, "If you forgive men their trespasses, your heavenly Father will also forgive you your trespasses; but if you do not forgive, neither will your Father forgive you your trespasses." This is said by Truth, deny it if it's not true. If you are a Christian and believe Christ, it's he who said, "I am the truth." What he says is true; it's sure.

Now listen to those who *speak the language of the world*: "Aren't you going to have your revenge? Will you let him tell others what he's done to you? Let him know he's dealing with a man!" These things are said everyday by people who *speak the language of the world; and the world listens to them.* Only those who love the world speak this way, and it's only those who love the world who listen to them. And you've heard that those who love the world and have no regard for love deny that Jesus came in the flesh. Did the Lord himself, in his flesh, do this? When he was struck, did he want to avenge himself? Did he not say, when he hung on the cross, "Father, forgive them, for they know not what they do"? If he who had power didn't use threats, why do you who are in someone else's power flare up? He died because he willed it, and he made no threats. You don't know when you'll die, and are you making threats?

We are of God. Let us see why, let us see whether it is for any reason other than love. *We are of God. Whoever knows God listens to us, and he who is not of God does not listen to us. By this we know the spirit of truth and the spirit of error.* He means that whoever listens to us has the spirit of truth, and whoever does not listen to us has the spirit of error. Let us see what counsel he is giving us. Let us listen to him counseling us in the spirit of truth, rather than listen to the antichrists, to lovers of the world.

Beloved, let us love one another. Why? Because some human being says so? No, *because love is of God.* This is a strong commendation of love, to say that it is *of God.* But he is going to say more: let us listen very carefully. *Love,* he has said, *is of God; and everyone who loves is born of God and knows God. One who does not love does not know God.* Why? *Because God is love.* What more could he say, dear friends? If there were nothing else in praise of love in all the pages of John's letter, nothing else whatever on any other page of Scripture, and if we heard only this one thing from the voice of God's Spirit, that *God is love,* we should ask for nothing more.

Now you see that to act contrary to love is to act contrary to God. None of you should say, "I'm sinning against a human being when I don't love my sister or brother. To sin against another person isn't much; it's only against God I shouldn't sin!" But how is it you don't sin against God when you sin against love? *God is love.* These aren't my words. If I said that *God is love,* any of you might be offended and ask, "What did he say? What did he mean, *God is love?* God gave love, God bestowed love." *Love is of God. . . . God is love.* This is God's Scripture, dear friends. This letter is canonical; all peoples read it. It's held by universal authority, it has edified the whole earth. It's God's Spirit that tells you here that *God is love.* Now, if you dare, go against God and refuse to love your sister and brother!

Love is of God; and *God is love.* God is Father, Son, and Holy Spirit. The Son is God from God; the Holy Spirit is God from God. And these three are one God, not three gods. If the Son is God, and the Holy Spirit is God, and those in whom the Holy Spirit dwells love others, then love is God.

It *is* God because *of* God. Both things are said in this letter: *Love is of God* and *God is love.* Only of the Father does Scripture never say that he is of God. When you hear *of God,* you have to think of the Son or the Holy Spirit. But because the Apostle says that "God's love has been poured out in our hearts through the Holy Spirit which has been given to us," we must understand that in love is the Holy Spirit. The Holy Spirit, which the wicked can't receive, is that fountain of which Scripture says, "Let your fountain of water be your own, and let no stranger partake of it with you." All those who don't love God are strangers, antichrists. They may enter our churches, but they can't be counted among the children of God. That fountain of life doesn't belong to them. The wicked too can have baptism; they can have the gift of prophecy. King Saul had the gift of prophecy. He persecuted David, who was innocent, and he began to prophesy. The wicked too can receive the sacrament of the Lord's body and blood. Of such people it is said that "anyone who eats and drinks unworthily eats and drinks judgment on himself." The wicked too can have the name of Christ; they can be called Christians. It was said of them that "they defiled the name of their God." The wicked too can share in all these mysteries, these sacraments, but to have love and to be wicked isn't possible. This is the Spirit's special gift; the Spirit is the one and only fountain. God's Spirit urges you to drink of it; God's Spirit urges you to drink of himself.

15. God Has Loved Us First (1 John 4:9–12)

God is love. In this the love of God was made manifest among us, that he sent his only Son into this world, so that we might live through him. As the Lord himself said, "Greater love than this no one can have, that he lay down his life for his friends." Christ's love for us was proven in that he died for us. How is the Father's love for us proven? In that he sent his only Son to die for us. So too Paul the apostle says, "He who did not spare his own Son but gave him up for us all, has he not given us all things with him?"

The Father "gave up" Christ, and so did Judas. Does it seem as if they did the same thing? Judas is a betrayer. Is God the Father also a betrayer? "Of course not!" you say. But it's the Apostle who says it best: "He who did not spare his own Son but *gave him up* for us all. . . . " The Father gave up his Son, and the Son gave himself up. The same Apostle writes of "the Son of God who loved me and gave himself up for me." If the Father gave up his Son, and the Son gave himself up, what did Judas do? What is it that distinguishes the Father giving up his Son, the Son giving up himself, and Judas the disciple giving up his Master? This is the difference: what the Father and the Son did in love, Judas did in treachery.

You see that it's not what people do that you have to consider, but the mind and intention with which they do it. We find God the Father and Judas doing one and the same thing. We bless the Father yet we detest Judas. Why do we bless the Father but detest Judas? We bless love, we detest wickedness. How great is the good that has come to the human race from the giving up of Christ! Was this what Judas was thinking of when he betrayed him? In the mind of God was the salvation by which we were redeemed, but Judas thought of the price he got for his Lord. The Son had in mind the price he paid for us, and Judas the price he got for selling him. A difference in intention renders a difference in the deeds. The deed is one and the same, but if we measure it by the different intentions we find one thing to love and one to condemn, one to glorify and one to abhor. This is the power of love. Only love discriminates, only love distinguishes between human actions.

I've been speaking of similar actions. When they are different, we find that love makes one person fierce, and wickedness makes another charming and seductive. A parent may strike a child and a kidnapper may caress it. If you offered a choice between the two things, blows and caresses, who wouldn't choose caresses and run away from the blows? But if you look at the people they come from, it's love that strikes the blows and wickedness that offers the caresses. Do you see what I'm saying? Human actions can be distinguished only by the love in which they are rooted. There are many things that look good but don't come from the root of love. Thorns too have their flowers: some acts seem harsh and cruel, but they are done for the sake of discipline, and the motive is love. Once and for all, I give you a short precept: Love, and do what you will. If you keep silent, keep silent out of love. If you raise your voice, raise it out of love. If you correct, correct out of love. If you leave alone, leave alone out of love. Have love's root within you; nothing but good can spring from this root.

In this the love of God was made manifest among us, that he sent his only Son into this world, so that we might live through him. In this is love, not that we loved God, but that he loved us. We didn't love him first; he loved us so that we would love him. *And he sent his Son as the Atoner for our sins.* The atoner is the one who offers the sacrifice. He offered a sacrifice for our sins. Where did he find the sacrifice, the pure victim he would offer? Because he found nothing else, he offered himself.

Beloved, if God so loved us we also ought to love one another. "Peter," Jesus said, "do you love me?" And he answered, "I do love you." "Feed my sheep," Jesus responded.

No one has ever seen God. God is an invisible reality. We must seek him with our hearts, not our eyes. But just as when we want to see the physical sun we cleanse our eyes, which are our means of seeing it, so also if we want to see God we have to cleanse the eyes which can see him. Which are these eyes? Listen to the gospel: "Blessed are the pure in heart, for they shall see God." But you mustn't imagine God to yourselves according to what your eyes desire. You may represent to yourselves a huge shape or some measureless immensity spread out in space like the physical light before our eyes, which you enlarge as much as you can in all directions. Or you may picture him as an old man of venerable appearance. But don't think this way. The following will give you a true idea, if you want to see God: "God is love." What is love's face like? What is its shape, its size? What kind of hands and feet does it have? No one can say. And yet it has feet, for they lead us to church; it has hands, for they reach out to the poor; it has eyes, for they consider the needy: "Blessed is he who considers the needy and poor," as the psalm says. We know it has ears, because the Lord says of them: "He who has ears to hear, let him hear." These aren't parts set in different places; the person who has love sees the whole at once by thought. Live in love and love will live in you; abide in love and love will abide in you.

But what do you say, my friends, is there anyone who loves what he doesn't see? Take yourselves: why, when you hear love praised, do you stand up and shout out your praise? What have I shown you? Have I produced any colors? Or displayed gold and silver before your eyes? Or dug precious stones out of a treasure? Have I shown you anything like this? Has my face changed while I've been speaking? My body looks the same as it did when I came in, and so do your bodies. Love is praised and you shout applause. Certainly there's nothing for you to see. But as you delight to hear love praised, take delight too in preserving it in your hearts.

Listen to me, dear friends. I exhort you, with the strength God gives me, to seek this great treasure. If someone showed you a little vase of wrought gold, made perfectly at great cost, which charmed you and made you want it, and if the artist's work and the weight of the metal and its luster delighted you, wouldn't every one of you say, "Oh, if I had that vase!" And it wouldn't do you any good to say it, because it wouldn't be in your power to possess it. Or if one of you wanted to have it, you'd have to think of stealing it from someone else's house. But you hear love praised, and if you want it, it is yours. You possess it. You don't need to steal it or buy it; it's free. Take it and embrace it; there is nothing more delightful. If love is as I say when it's only spoken of, ponder what it is like when you possess it.

If any of you want to preserve love, my friends, above all you must keep from thinking that it is something poor and inactive. Love isn't preserved by that kind of meekness which is really laziness and indifference. That's not the way. Don't think you're loving your servants when you never beat them, or your children when you never discipline them, or your neighbors when you never find fault with them. That isn't love, it's weakness. Let your love be zealous to reprove and correct. Be pleased by good behavior, correct and reprove what is bad. Don't love anyone's error but love the person. It's the person that God made, while we make our own errors. Love what God made, don't love what we ourselves have done. When you love the person, you remove the error; when you esteem the person, you correct the fault. If sometimes you have to be severe, let it be for love of what is better.

That is why love was made manifest by the dove that descended upon the Lord. In the form of a dove the Holy Spirit, the one who pours out love in us, came. And why was that? Because the dove has no gall. It fights for its nest with beak and wings, but its violence is without bitterness. This is how parents act too. When they chastise their children, they do it for the sake of discipline. As I said, a kidnapper who would sell a child seduces it with bitterness; a parent who would correct a child chastises it without gall. You must be like this with everyone. My friends, here you have a good example, a good rule. All of you have children or want to have them; or if you've decided to have no children of your body, you want spiritual children. Do any of you not correct your children? Are there any of you whom your parents don't discipline? No doubt they seem severe. Love is severe, but it is a severity without gall, like the dove's, not like the raven's.

16. Caring for Love

Love is a delightful word, but the thing itself is even more delightful. I can't be speaking of it all the time. I have much to do, and my various activities distract me so that I'm not always at leisure to speak of love, even though there is nothing better I could do. But even if I can't always be speaking of it, I can always keep it in myself. It's like the "Alleluia" we sing during Eastertide. Singing "Alleluia" lasts only a few moments, and we go on to something else. *Alleluia* means "praise God," you know. You can't always be praising God in words, but you can always praise him by your way of life.

Works of mercy, loving affections, holy piety, unshakable chastity, unassuming temperance: these you should always keep, in public or at home, when you're with others or when you're alone, speaking or silent, busy or at leisure. You should keep them continually, because all these virtues I've named are interior ones. But who's competent to name them all? They're like a general's army inside your heart. A general does whatever he decides through his army, and in the same way our Lord Jesus Christ employs these virtues as his servants once he begins to live in our "inner self," "in our hearts, through faith." These virtues are invisible, but we praise them when we speak of them. We wouldn't do this if we didn't love them, and we wouldn't love them if we didn't see them. But if this is true, then we do see them, but with other eyes, with the inner vision of the heart. By the invisible virtues I've mentioned, we visibly move our members. Our feet walk but where do they go? Wherever our good will, serving a good general, moves them. Our hands work but what do they do? They do whatever love commands of them, whatever the love of the Holy Spirit inspires in them. We see our members only when they move; we don't see who commands them from within. And who this is can be known only to the One who commands and to the one who is inwardly commanded.

Dear friends, do you remember the words of the gospel, "Beware of practicing your righteousness before men in order to be seen by them"? Does our Lord mean that we should hide the good we do from other people and fear to be seen by them? If you don't have any onlookers, you won't have any imitators. Therefore you should be seen. But you're not to do good in order to be seen. That shouldn't be the cause of your happiness, the reason you rejoice, so that you suppose you've obtained all the fruit of your good deed when you've been seen and praised. That's nothing. Consider yourself unworthy when you're praised, and let the One who works through you be praised in you. Don't do good so you'll be praised; rather do it for the glory of the One who makes it possible for you to do good. From yourself comes your power of doing wrong, from God your power of doing right.

See how foolish are the people who think otherwise! The good they do they attribute to themselves, and they want to blame God when they do wrong. I don't know what to call this distorted and irrational attitude, which turns things on their heads. We must set things aright! Do you want to have God underneath and yourself on top? That's putting yourself down, not up! God is always on top. Is it that you do right and God wrong? Say this instead, if you want to speak the truth: "I do wrong and he does right; and the good I do comes from him, because all I do on my own is bad." This confession strengthens your heart and provides a firm foundation for love.

This is what I say, then, my friends, and I wouldn't stop saying it even if I could. Let your actions be those that are appropriate to the season, the hour, the day. Should you always be speaking or silent or resting or fasting? Always giving bread to the needy? Always clothing the naked? Always visiting the sick? Always reconciling those having a quarrel? Always burying the dead? No, now you should do one thing, now another.

These actions have a beginning and an end. But the principle that commands them doesn't begin, and it must not stop. The love within you shouldn't cease. Love's services must be done at the appropriate time.

17. Love of Our Enemies

Some of you may have been wondering, while I've been commenting on this letter of John's, why the thing he especially urges on us is love of our sisters and brothers. He speaks of "one who loves his brother," and he says, "This is his commandment, that we should love one another." He's always talking about love of our sisters and brothers. Love of God— that is, the love we must have for God—he doesn't mention as often, but it's there. But love of our enemies is scarcely mentioned anywhere in the whole letter. Although he eagerly preaches love to us and urges it on us, he doesn't tell us to love our enemies; rather, he tells us to love our sisters and brothers. Now in the gospel we hear, "For if you love those who love you, what reward have you? Do not even the tax collectors do the same?" How is it that John the apostle urges fraternal love on us as a great point of perfection, and the Lord tells us that this is not enough, that we have to enlarge our love so that it reaches even to our enemies?

Those who love their enemies don't disregard their sisters and brothers. Love is like fire: first it has to seize what's close by, and then it stretches out to what is farther away. Your sisters and brothers are closer to you than anyone else. Again, a person you don't know but who doesn't oppose you is closer to you than an enemy, who does oppose you. Extend your love to the people close to you, but don't call it an extension. It's almost loving yourself when you love those attached to you. Extend it further to people you don't know, people who haven't done you any harm. But go beyond them too; go on and love your enemies. This is clearly what the Lord commands. But why hasn't John said anything about loving our enemies?

All love, my friends, even what is called carnal love, contains a certain goodwill toward those who are loved. We shouldn't love human beings as we hear gluttons say that they "love" pheasant. Ask them why they love to kill and consume them! They say they love them, but the result is death for the pheasants. What we love to eat we love for this reason: to consume it and be refreshed. Are we to love human beings as things to be consumed?

There's a certain friendliness, a goodwill, that leads us at times to do good to those we love. What if there's nothing we can do? Goodwill alone is enough for a lover. We shouldn't wish people to be wretched so that we can perform the works of mercy. You give bread to the hungry, but it would be better if no one was hungry and you had no one to give to. You clothe the naked, but if only everyone had clothes and you didn't need to! You bury the dead, yet I wish that time were here when no one dies! You reconcile those who are quarreling, but we long for the eternal peace of Jerusalem, when there will be no discord! All these are our responses to needs. Take away the wretched and works of mercy will cease. Works of mercy will cease, but does that mean the flame of love will go out? No, the love you have for a fortunate person, to whom you have nothing you can give, is a fuller and truer love; it's purer and far more sincere. If you do good to some wretched person, you may want to exalt yourself and have the object of your good deed under obligation to you. Say there is someone in need, and you share what you have. Because you're the giver you feel superior to the one who receives your gift. You should want to be equal, so that you may both be subject to the One to whom nothing can be given.

A Christian must be one who does not set himself up over other human beings. It's by God's gift that you are superior to the beasts and better than they are. This you possess by nature. You'll always be better than a beast. If you want to be better than some other person, you'll be envious when you see that you're equal. If you surpass someone in wisdom, you ought to want that one—say some man—to be wise too. As long as you're ahead he learns from you; while he's ignorant he needs you. You'll appear to be the teacher and he the learner. Because you're the teacher you're superior to him, and as the learner he's inferior. Unless you want him to be your equal, you'll want him always to be learning from you. And if this is what you want, you'll be an envious teacher. If you're an envious teacher, how will you be a teacher at all? So I beg you, don't teach him your envy! Listen to the Apostle speaking from the heart of love: "I wish that all were as I myself am!" Do you see how he wanted all to be his equals? It is because love made him want this that he was superior to them all.

Show mercy, then, as do people with merciful hearts, because even in loving your enemies you are loving your sisters and brothers. Don't think that John has given no commandment concerning love of enemies. He's spoken of the love of sisters and brothers, and it's always them you are loving. Do you ask how this comes about? I ask you: Why should you love your enemies? Is it for the sake of good health in this life? What if that's not expedient? Do you want them to be rich? What if they'll be blinded by their riches? Do you want them married? What if this makes their lives bitter? Do you want them to have children? What if they turn out badly? These things that you appear to desire for your enemies because you love them are uncertain. Desire for them rather that they share eternal life with you. Desire that they be your sisters and brothers. If this is what you desire when you love your enemies, that they be your sisters and brothers, then when you love them it's sisters and brothers you are loving. It is not what they are that you love in them but what you would have them be.

Imagine, my friends, that there's a tree trunk lying in front of you. A skillful craftsman sees it, unhewn, just as it was cut down in the forest, and takes a liking to it. He wants to make something out of it: this is why he likes it; he doesn't just want to leave it as it is. By his craft he sees what it will be, and this is what he likes, not what it is in its present state. This is the way God has loved us sinners. I say, God has loved sinners, for he said that "those who are well don't need a physician, rather those who are sick." Did he love us when we were sinners so that we'd continue to be sinners? It's as the craftsman looked on the tree from the forest that our Craftsman looked on us: what he saw was not the raw material but the edifice he was going to make of it. This is the way you too must look on your enemies, those who oppose you, who rage against you, who wound you with their words and provoke you with their slanders, who harass you with their hatred. You must remember that these are human beings. You see in all their hostility to you their own doing, while you see in them as persons God's doing. That your enemies are human is God's doing; their hatred, their malice, these are their own doings. And what do you say in your heart? "Lord, be merciful to them, forgive them their sins, put fear in them, change them!" It's not what they are that you love in them but what you would have them be. So when you love your enemies, you are loving your sisters and brothers.

Therefore, perfect love is the love of your enemies, and this perfect love consists in the love of your sisters and brothers. You can't say that John the apostle has insisted less on this point than Christ our Lord: John has told us to love our sisters and brothers; Christ has told us to love even our enemies. But notice the reason Christ has told us to love our enemies. Is it that they'll always be our enemies? If this was why he said what he did, you'd be hating them, not loving them. Consider his own love. He didn't want his persecutors to remain his persecutors: "Father," he said, "forgive them, for they know not what they do." By wanting them to be forgiven, he wanted them to be changed; he wanted his enemies made into his brothers, and this is truly what he did. He was killed and buried; he arose, ascended into heaven, and sent the Holy Spirit to his disciples. They began boldly to preach his name; they performed miracles in the name of the One who was crucified and slain. The Lord's slayers saw these things, and the blood they had shed in their rage they came to drink in faith.

18. Abiding in God
(1 John 4:12-16)

No one has ever seen God. See, my friends: *If we love one another, God will abide in us and his love will be perfected in us.* Begin to love and you'll be made perfect. Have you begun to love? Then God has begun to dwell in you. Love him who's begun to dwell in you, so that by dwelling more perfectly in you he'll make you perfect. *By this we know that we abide in him and he in us, because he has given to us of his own Spirit.* Good! Thanks be to God! We know that he dwells in us. How do we know it? Because John has told us that *he has given to us of his own Spirit.* And how do you know that he's given to you of his own Spirit? Ask your hearts. If they're filled with love, then you have the Spirit of God. And how do we know that this is the sign that God's Spirit dwells in you? Ask the apostle Paul: "Because God's love has been poured out in our hearts through the Holy Spirit which has been given to us."

And we have seen and bear witness that the Father has sent his Son, the Saviour of the world. Don't be anxious, you who are sick. Do you give up hope when such a Physician has come? Your diseases were grave, your wounds incurable, your sickness desperate. Do you see only the greatness of your troubles and not the almighty power of the Doctor? You are desperate but he is almighty. His witnesses are those who were healed at the first and now proclaim the Doctor. But even they were healed more in hope than in reality, as the Apostle says: "For in hope we are saved." So we've begun to be healed in faith, and our healing will be perfected when this corruptible nature shall have put on incorruption, and this mortal nature shall have put on immortality. That's hope, it isn't yet the reality. But those who rejoice in hope will possess the reality too; no one without hope will be able to come to the reality.

Whoever confesses that Jesus is the Son of God, God abides in him and he in God. Let me say it briefly: this confession must be in deeds, not words; made not by tongues but by lives. There are many people who profess their faith in words but deny it by their actions. *And we have known and believed the love God has for us.* And again, how have you known it? *God is love.* John told us this earlier; now he says it again. There's nothing greater he could say about love than to say that it is God. You may have been ready to think little of God's gift, but will you despise God? *God is love, and he who abides in love abides in God, and God abides in him.* There is a mutual indwelling of the One who holds and the one who is held. You dwell in God so that you're held by him; God dwells in you to hold you, to keep you from falling. Don't think of yourself as being God's house in the way that your house supports your body. If that house stops supporting you, you fall; but he doesn't fall if you stop supporting him. He's whole when you forsake him, and he's whole when you return to him. Your healing is not gain to him; it's you who are purified, recreated, straightened out. He's medicine for the ill, a straight rule for the crooked, a light for the darkened, a home for the homeless. Everything works to your advantage. Don't imagine that you're conferring some advantage on God when you come to him, even with a promise to belong to him. Will God lack servants if you refuse, if everyone refuses? God doesn't need servants! But his servants need him. That's why the psalmist says, "I have said to the Lord, you are my God"—he is the true Lord—"because you have no need of my goods." You are different: you need the goods other people provide for you, and they need what you provide for them. Therefore you're no true lord, because you need an inferior. That One is our true Lord who seeks nothing from us. And woe to us if we don't seek him! There's nothing he seeks from us, but he sought us even when we weren't seeking him. One sheep strayed and he found it and brought it back on his shoulders rejoicing. Was the sheep necessary to the shepherd? Wasn't it the shepherd who was necessary to the sheep?

I get so much pleasure speaking about love that I don't want this letter of John's to end. There's nothing in Scripture that speaks of love more warmly, and nothing more delightful to preach to you or more wholesome for you to take in. But this is on the condition that you confirm God's gift in yourselves by your good lives. Don't be ungrateful for this great grace he's given you. God had an Only Son, but not wanting him to be alone, he adopted us so that he would have sisters and brothers to possess with him life everlasting.

19. Confidence for the Day of Judgment (1 John 4:17)

My friends, you remember that I still have the last part of John's letter to expound to you, as the Lord gives me the grace. I haven't forgotten my debt, and you shouldn't forget to claim it. The love that is the main and almost the sole subject of this letter makes me faithful in acknowledging my debt, and you kind and gentle in claiming it. Where love is lacking demands are bitter, but when it is present they are welcome. And even though the one on whom they are made has to undertake some labor, still love makes this work light and almost nothing. Don't we see the same thing in dumb and irrational animals? Their love isn't spiritual; it's carnal and natural. Yet we see how insistently the young claim their milk from their mother's breasts. The sucklings may treat their mother roughly, but she likes this better than if they don't suck, if they don't claim what love owes them. Don't we often see a half-grown calf butt its mother's udder with its head and almost lift her off the ground? Yet it's not kicked away. On the contrary, if the young one isn't there to suck, the mother lows to it to come. The Apostle says of spiritual love, "I became little among you, like a nurse cherishing her children." If this love is in me, then I love you when you claim your due. But those who are lazy I don't love, because I am afraid for them.

In this is love perfected in us, that we may have confidence for the day of judgment, because as he is so are we in this world. John is telling us how each one of us may test love's progress in us; or rather, our progress in love. For if God is love, and if God

knows neither progress nor decline, then we say that love is
making progress in you only to the extent that you are making progress in love. Ask, then, how you are progressing in
love, and to learn the measure of your progress, listen to what
your heart replies.

John promised to show us how we may know this when he
said, *In this is love perfected in us.* Ask him, In what? *That we
may have confidence for the day of judgment.* Love is perfected in
the person who has confidence for the day of judgment. And
what does this mean? It means that we aren't afraid of its
coming. There are people who don't believe in a day of judgment; they can't have confidence for a day they don't believe
will come. We can leave them aside. May God awaken them
to life! I have nothing to say about the dead; they neither fear
nor desire what they don't believe in.

There are others who have begun to believe in a day of
judgment, and with their belief comes fear. Because they are
afraid, they don't yet have confidence for the day of judgment, and love isn't yet perfect in them. But they mustn't lose
hope. If someone's made a beginning, why despair of the end?
But what is the beginning I see? It's fear. Listen to Scripture:
"The fear of the Lord is the beginning of wisdom." People
who've begun to fear the day of judgment must amend themselves in their fear. They must keep watch against their enemies, their sins. They must begin to renew the life within
them and to mortify their "members which are on earth," as
the Apostle tells us. By the "members which are on earth" he
means "the spiritual hosts of wickedness" as he explains,
naming greediness and impurity and others. Now the more
those who've begun to fear the day of judgment mortify their
members which are on earth, the more their heavenly members rise and gain strength. These heavenly members are all
the different kinds of good works, and as their heavenly
members rise up they begin to desire what they once feared.
They were afraid that Christ would come and find them godless people, whom he'd condemn; now they are eager for his

coming, because he'll find holy people, whom he'll crown! When their chaste souls have begun to long for Christ's coming and for their Bridegroom's embrace, they renounce all adulterous loves. Faith, hope, and love make them inwardly virgin. Now they have confidence for the day of judgment. They experience no inner conflict when they pray, "thy kingdom come!" Those who fear the coming of God's kingdom are afraid this prayer will be heard. But how can people be said to pray who are afraid that their prayer will be heard? Those who pray with the confidence of love now truly desire that the kingdom will come. It was with this desire that the psalmist said, "And you, O Lord, how long? Turn, Lord, and deliver my soul." He was distressed that it was delayed. There are people who die with patience; and there are some, those who are perfect, who live with patience.

Let me explain what I mean by this. Those who still want this life patiently endure the day of death when it comes. They struggle against themselves in order to follow God's will, and to act according to God's choice and not their human will. But their desire for this present life causes them to struggle with death, and it takes patience and fortitude for them to die with an untroubled spirit. These people die patiently. But those who desire, as the Apostle says, "to depart and be with Christ" don't die with patience, they live with patience and die with delight. Look at the Apostle, not loving life here but bearing it with patience: "To depart," he says, "and be with Christ is far better; but to remain in the flesh is necessary on your account."

So, my friends, set to work and train yourselves to desire the day of judgment. Your only proof of perfect love is that you've begun to long for this day. To long for it is to have confidence for it, and to have confidence for it means that your conscience in its perfect and sincere love feels no alarm.

In this is love perfected in us, that we may have confidence for the day of judgment. Why will we have confidence? *Because as he is,* John says, *so are we in this world.* Do you think he's said something impossible? Can a human being be as God is? I've already explained that *as* doesn't always signify equality but sometimes only a certain likeness. For example, as you have two ears so has your image; the two cases are not the same, but you still say *as*. Thus because we were made in God's image we are "as" God; that is we are not his equals, but we are like him according to our measure.

Then where does our confidence for the day of judgment come from? *Because as he is so are we in this world.* We must understand this in reference to love. The Lord says in the gospel, "If you love those who love you, what reward have you? Do not even the tax collectors do the same?" What does he want us to do, then? "But I say to you, love your enemies and pray for those who persecute you." If he's commanding us to love our enemies, what example does he give us? It's God himself: "So that you may be children of your Father who is in heaven." And what does God do? He loves his enemies: "He makes his sun rise on the good and on the wicked, and sends his rain on the just and on the unjust." And so the perfection God calls us to is to love our enemies as he loves his own, and our confidence for the day of judgment is *because as he is so are we in this world*. As he loves his enemies, making his sun to rise on the good and the wicked and sending his rain on the just and the unjust, so, even though we can't give sun and rain to our enemies, we can give them our tears when we pray for them.

20. Love Casts Out Fear (1 John 4:18)

Let us look now at what John says about confidence. How are we to recognize that love is perfect? *There is no fear in love.* Then what shall we say of those who have begun to fear the day of judgment? If their love were perfect, they wouldn't feel any fear. Perfect love would produce perfect righteousness, and they would have no reason to fear. Instead they'd have reason to desire that wickedness pass away and God's kingdom come. So *there is no fear in love.* But this is not true of love that has only begun to exist. Of what love is it true, then? *But perfect love,* John says, *casts out fear.* Fear, then, is the beginning, because "the fear of the Lord is the beginning of wisdom." Fear, we may say, prepares a place for love, but when love begins to dwell there, the fear that has prepared the place for it is driven out. As the one grows the other decreases; as love becomes more interior, fear is driven outside. The more love there is, the less fear; the less love, the more fear.

But if there is no fear, there is no way love can come in. When we sew something we use a needle to introduce the thread. The needle goes in first, but it has to come out if the thread is to follow. In the same way fear first occupies our minds. But it doesn't remain there, because it only enters to introduce love. And once security is established in our souls, what joy we have in this world and in the world to come! Even in this world, who can harm us if we are filled with love? Listen to the Apostle rejoicing in love: "Who will separate us from the love of Christ?" he asks. "Shall tribulation, or distress, or persecution, or famine, or nakedness, or peril, or the sword?" And Peter: "And who is there who can harm you if you are zealous for what is good?"

There is no fear in love, but perfect love casts out fear because fear has to do with torment. The consciousness of sins torments the heart. Justification hasn't yet been accomplished, and there's something there that irritates and stings. Accordingly, what does the psalmist say concerning the perfection of justice? "You have turned for me my mourning into gladness; you have stripped off my sackcloth and girded me with joy, so that my glory may sing to you and I may not be stung by remorse." What does this last phrase mean? It means that my conscience is untroubled. Fear does trouble it but then love comes in and heals the wound fear has made. Fear of God wounds like a surgeon's knife; it cuts out the festering part and seems to enlarge the wound. While the festering remained in the body, the wound was smaller but dangerous. Then comes the surgeon's knife, and the pain is greater now as he opens the wound. The treatment is more painful than leaving it alone, but the added pain of the treatment serves to end pain by restoring health. Let fear occupy your hearts, then, so that love can enter them. A healing scar follows the surgeon's knife. But our Physician is such that no scars appear! Just submit to his hand. If you are without fear you cannot be justified; there's a line of Scripture that says this. Fear must enter first so that love can come in. Fear is the treatment, love is health. *One who fears is not perfected* in love. This is *because fear has to do with torment,* just like the surgeon's incision.

But there is another line of Scripture that seems to contradict this one, unless it's rightly understood. In a certain place in the psalms it is said, "The fear of the Lord is pure, enduring forever." The psalmist is telling us of a fear that is eternal but pure. But if he's showing us an eternal fear, isn't John contradicting him when he says that *there is no fear in love, but perfect love casts out fear?*

Let us examine these two words of God. Even if there are two books, two mouths, two tongues, there is only one Spirit. One of these words is John's, one is David's. But don't think that the Spirit is more than one. If one breath can fill twin pipes, can't one Spirit fill two hearts and move two tongues? And if twin pipes filled by a single breath blend, can two voices moved by God's breath be out of harmony? There must then be some agreement, some harmony, in these texts, but we have to be able to listen.

We must look at the difference between the two fears, and thereby comprehend the harmony of the twin pipes. How are we to understand and distinguish between them? Dear friends, listen. There are people who fear God because they fear being cast into hell to burn with the devil in eternal fire. This the fear that introduces love, but it only enters to go out again. If you still fear God on account of the punishment you may receive from him, then you aren't yet loving him. You're not longing for good things, but trying to avoid bad ones. Then because you want to escape evils, you amend yourself and begin to desire good things. And when you do this, it will be a pure fear that is in you. But what is this pure fear? It's a fear of losing what is good. Notice this: it's one thing to fear God because he may send you to hell with the devil, and another to fear him lest he forsake you. The first kind isn't yet pure; it doesn't come from love of God but from fear of punishment. Only when you fear God lest his presence leave you are you embracing him and longing to enjoy him.

I don't think I can show the difference between these two kinds of fear, the one that love casts out and the pure fear that endures forever, better than by comparing two married women. Suppose that one of them wants to commit adultery. She enjoys her wicked desire, but she's afraid that her husband will accuse her. She fears her husband but her fear comes from her love of wickedness. Her husband's presence is no pleasure to her but a burden, and if she lives sinfully she fears his coming. People who fear the day of judgment are like this woman. But imagine another woman, one who loves her husband. She keeps herself for him, never staining her mind with adulterous thoughts. This woman longs for her husband's presence. And how does this help us to distinguish between the two kinds of fear? Ask both of the women whether they are afraid, and they will give you exactly the same answer. They say the same words, but their thoughts are different. Ask them again, and this time ask them why they are afraid. One will tell you that she fears her husband's coming, and the other that she fears her husband's going. One is afraid of being accused, the other of being left alone. Now apply this distinction to Christian hearts, and you will find one fear that love casts out and another fear that is pure and that endures forever.

Let me speak first to those people who fear God like the woman who enjoys wickedness and is afraid her husband may accuse her. Souls, as you feel aversion to this woman, feel aversion to yourselves! If you have husbands or wives, do you want them to fear your accusations? Do you want them to enjoy their wickedness and be restrained only by their fear of you, not by their hatred of evil? Wouldn't you rather they were chaste from love of you and not from fear? Then show yourselves to God as you want them to be to you. And for the unmarried who want to marry, this is the kind of spouse you should want.

Let me explain, my friends. Perhaps the woman who fears her husband because he may accuse her doesn't commit adultery just because her husband might find it out and deprive her of light and life. Perhaps she can fool him, for he's only human, just as she is. Still she's afraid of him, even though she can escape discovery. And you, don't you fear the eyes of the One no one can deceive? Or the presence of the One who can't be turned away from you? Beseech God to look upon you and to turn his face away from your sins. But how might you deserve to have him do this? It's if you don't turn your own face away. As the psalm says, it's "because I know my iniquity, and my sin is ever before me." Feel misgiving for yourself and he will be forgiving toward you.

I've been talking to those souls who still have the fear that doesn't endure forever, the fear that love casts out. Now I'll address those who already have a pure fear, the fear that endures forever. Do you think I'll find any like that to address? Any among our people? In this church? On this earth? There must be but they are hidden. It's winter and the greenness is inside, in the root. Perhaps my words are reaching their ears. But wherever they may be, I wish I could find them, and instead of having them listen to me I'd listen to them. Those souls would teach me rather than learn from me. A holy soul, a soul on fire with longing for God's kingdom: it's not I who speak to this soul but God himself. This is how he consoles it as it lives in patience on this earth: "Already you want me to come, and I know that this is what you want. I know what you are, that you are waiting without anxiety for my coming. I know this is troubling to you, but continue your waiting and be patient: I come, and I come quickly." But time moves slowly for a loving soul. Listen to it singing like a lily among thorns: "I will sing, and I will give heed in a way that is blameless: 'When will you come to me?' " In the "way that is blameless" there is no need for fear, because *perfect love casts out fear.* But even when this soul comes to its Spouse's embrace it will fear—but in peace. What will it fear then? It will take care to guard itself from its iniquity lest it sin again. It won't fear being cast into everlasting fire, but it will fear being forsaken by God. In that soul there will be "a pure fear, enduring forever."

We've been listening to two pipes playing in harmony. Both tell of fear: one of the fear of being accused, the other of the fear of being forsaken. One is the fear that love excludes, the other the fear that endures forever.

21. God First Loved Us
(1 John 4:19-21)

Let us love, because he first loved us. How would we be able to love if he hadn't first loved us? It's by loving that we became his friends, even though it was as his enemies that he loved us in order that we might become his friends. He loved us first and gave us the gift of loving him. By loving we became beautiful. What does a man who is ugly and misshapen do if he loves a beautiful woman? And what does an ugly woman do if she loves a handsome man? Can loving make her beautiful? Or can the man by loving become handsome? He's in love with a beautiful woman, but when he looks at himself in the mirror, he's ashamed to show his face to the beauty he loves. What can he do to become handsome? Should he wait for good looks to come? Waiting brings only old age, which makes him uglier. There's nothing he can do, there's no advice you can give him except to restrain himself and not to venture to love someone so much better looking than himself.

Through iniquity our souls, my friends, are loathsome. In loving God they become beautiful. What a love it is that makes the lover beautiful! God is always beautiful, never ugly, never changeable. The One who is always beautiful loved us first, and what were we then when he loved us if not loathsome and ugly? But it wasn't to leave us loathsome that he loved us, but to change us and to make the ugly beautiful. How do we become beautiful? It's by loving him who is always beautiful. As love grows in you so does beauty, because love is the beauty of the soul.

Let us love, because he first loved us. Listen to Paul: "But God shows his love for us in that while we were yet sinners Christ died for us," a righteous man dying for the unrighteous, the beautiful dying for the loathsome. Where do we find that Jesus is beautiful? Look in the psalm: "You are the fairest of the children of men; grace is poured out upon your lips." What is the source of his beauty? "You are the fairest of the children of men" because "in the beginning was the Word, and the Word was with God, and the Word was God." When he took flesh it's as if he took on the loathsomeness that is our mortal state, in order to conform and identify himself with us, to excite us to love an inner beauty. We've found Jesus beautiful, "fairest of the children of men"! Where do we find that he is loathsome and ugly? Question the prophet Isaiah: "And we saw him, and he had no beauty nor comeliness."

Here are twin pipes that seem to be out of harmony, but still one Spirit breathes into them both. Don't turn away from the difficulty but apply yourselves. Let us question the apostle Paul, and listen to him explain the harmony of the twin pipes. "Though he was in the form of God, he did not count equality with God a thing to be grasped." There you see "the fairest of the children of men." "But he emptied himself, taking the form of a servant, being born in the likeness of men; and he was found in human form." "He had no beauty nor comeliness," and this was so that he might give them to you. What beauty and comeliness does he give you? Love. You already have this beauty. But don't look at yourself or you'll lose what you've received. Look toward him who made you beautiful. Be beautiful so that he'll love you. Turn your whole attention toward him, run toward him, seek his embraces, fear being separated from him. Have in yourselves that "pure fear that endures forever." *Let us love, because he first loved us.*

If anyone says, I love God. . . . Ask the people you meet whether they love God. They speak right up and profess, "I love him; he knows it." But you can ask in another way: *If anyone says, I love God, and hates his brother, he is a liar.* How do you show that he's a liar? Listen: *For he who does not love his brother whom he sees, how can he love God whom he does not see?* What then? Do those who love a sister or brother love God too? They must of necessity love God, they must of necessity love love itself. Is it possible for them to love a sister or brother and not love love? No, they have to love love. And so, because they love love, do they therefore love God? Of course! In loving love they love God. Or have you forgotten what we read a little while back, that "God is love"? If God is love, those who love love, love God. Love your sisters and brothers, then, and be at peace. You can't say, "I love my sister or my brother, but I don't love God." Just as you're lying if you say *I love God* when you don't love your sister or brother, so you're deceiving yourselves when you say, "I love my sister or brother," if you don't love God. If you love a sister or brother, you must love love itself. But "God is love." Therefore whoever loves a sister or brother must of necessity love God.

But if you don't love the sister or brother you see, how can you love the God you don't see? How can people not see God? It's because they don't have love. And the reason they don't have love is because they don't love their sister or brother. Therefore the reason they don't see God is because they lack love. If they have love they see God, because "God is love," and their inner eyes are purified more and more by love, so that they may see that unchangeable Being whose presence brings them unending joy and whom they will enjoy forever with the angels. But they must run now, so that one day they will rejoice in their own country. They aren't to love their journey or their route; they should find everything bitter except the One who calls them, until they hold him fast and say with the psalmist, "You have destroyed all those who commit fornication against you." And who are they who commit fornication? It's those who turn aside and love the world.

And what are you to do? What follows in the psalm: "But for me it is good to hold fast unto God." That is my whole good: to hold fast to God, without asking for recompense. For if you ask, "Why are you holding fast to God?" and someone says, "So that he'll give to me. . . " ask, "What will he give to you? It's God who made heaven, God who made the earth;

what is he going to give to you? You are already holding fast to
him; find something better, and he would give it to you!"

*For he who does not love his brother whom he sees, how can he love
God whom he does not see? And this commandment we have from
him, that he who loves God should love his brother also.* How grand-
ly you say that you love God; but you hate your brother! Murderer, how can you love God? Didn't you hear earlier in this
letter that "everyone who hates his brother is a murderer"?
You say, "But certainly I love God, even though I hate my
brother." And I answer, "Certainly you do *not* love God, if you
hate your brother!" I bring another proof. John has said that
Christ gave us a commandment, "that we love one another."
How can you love God when you hate his commandment?
Does anyone say, "I love our ruler but I hate his laws?" This is
how the ruler perceives whether you love him: if his laws are
observed throughout his empire. What is our Ruler's law? "A
new commandment I give you, that you love one another."
You tell me that you love Christ. Keep his law, then, and love
your sister and brother. If you don't love your sister and brother, how can you love him whose commandment you defy?

My friends, I never get tired of speaking about love in the
name of Christ. As for you, the more eager you are for it, the
more hope I have that it is increasing in you, and is casting out
fear, so that there may remain that pure fear that endures forever. Let us bear this world and its tribulations and the scandals
of our temptations. Let us never turn back from our way. Let us
hold to the unity of the Church, to Christ, to love. Let us not
be separated from the members of his Spouse or from the faith,
so that we may be glorified in his presence. In this way we will
abide securely in him, by faith now, and later by sight. It is his
great pledge we have, the gift of the Holy Spirit.

22. One Christ, Loving Himself (1 John 5:1–2)

Everyone who believes that Jesus is the Christ is born of God. Who are they who don't believe that Jesus is the Christ? It's those who don't live as Christ commanded. Many say that they believe, but faith without works doesn't save anyone. The work of faith is love. The apostle Paul puts it this way: "faith that works through love." That Jesus is the Christ is what they believe who are not Christians in name only but also in their deeds and their lives. This is not how the demons believe, for "the demons believe—and shudder," as Scripture tells us. What more could the demons believe than to say, "We know who you are, the Son of God." What the demons said, Peter said too: "You are the Christ, the Son of the living God." They used the same words, but their thoughts were different. How do we know that Peter was speaking with love? It's because a Christian's faith is accompanied by love and a demon's isn't. Peter said these words to embrace Christ; the demons said them to make Christ leave them. So you see, when John says *everyone who believes,* he means a particular kind of faith, not a faith held in common with many others. So, dear friends, don't let any heretic say to you, "We also believe." I've given you this example of the demons so that you won't be pleased with people's words but will look into their lives.

Let us see what it means to believe in Christ, to believe that Jesus is the Christ. *Everyone who believes that Jesus is the Christ is born of God.* But what does this belief mean? *And everyone who loves the parent loves the child.* John immediately links love and faith, because faith without love is empty. With love it's a Christian's faith, without love it's a demon's. As for those who don't believe at all, they're worse than demons, duller than demons. People who refuse to believe in Christ haven't even reached a demon's level. Others believe in Christ but hate him. They make a profession of faith because they are afraid of punishment, not because they love the prize. They are like the demons who are also afraid of being punished. Add love to this kind of faith, so that it will be the kind the apostle Paul describes, the "faith that works through love." Then you have a Christian, a citizen of Jerusalem and fellow citizen of the angels, a pilgrim sighing as he makes his way. Join this person, this companion of yours, and run together—if this is what you are too.

Everyone who loves the parent loves the child. Who is the parent? God the Father. Who is the child? It is the Son. What does John mean, then? That everyone who loves the Father loves the Son. *By this we know that we love the children of God.* What is John saying here, my friends? He was just speaking of God's *child,* his Son, not of his *children.* It's Christ alone that he set before us for our contemplation. Now he says, *By this we know that we love the children of God,* when we expect him to say "the Son of God." He now says *children of God,* even though he was just speaking of the Son of God, because *the children of God* are the body of God's Son. Because he is the Head and we are the members of his body, the Son of God is one. Therefore whoever loves God's children loves God's Son, and anyone who loves God's Son loves the Father. No one can love the Father without loving the Son, and anyone who loves the Son loves the children of God too.

What are these children of God? They are the members of God's Son. It is by loving that they become his members; through love they become part of Christ's bodily structure. Then there is one Christ, loving himself. For the love of the members for one another is the love of the body for itself. "If one member suffers, all the members suffer together; if one member is honored, all rejoice together." And what does Paul add to this? "Now you are the body of Christ and his members." John has just said to us regarding the love of our sisters and brothers, "He who does not love his brother whom he sees, how can he love God whom he does not see?" If you love your sister or brother, can you do this without loving Christ? How is this possible, when it's Christ's member you love? When you love his members you love Christ; when you love Christ you love God's Son; when you love God's Son you love the Father too. Love can't be divided into parts. Choose for yourself what you'll love, and you get the others too. If you say, "I love God alone, God the Father," you're not being truthful. If you love, you don't love him alone; if you love the Father you love the Son too. "Well," you say, "I love the Father and I love the Son, but that's all: God the Father; and God the Son, our Lord Jesus Christ, who ascended into heaven and sits at the right hand of the Father, the Word through whom everything was made, the Word that became flesh and dwelt among us. That's all I love." You're wrong again! If you love the Head you love the members too, and if you don't love the members neither do you love the Head. Don't you tremble when you hear the voice of the Head crying from heaven on behalf of his members, "Saul, Saul, why are you persecuting me?" He calls the one persecuting his members his own persecutor. He calls the one who loves his members a lover of himself. And you already know what his members are, my friends: the Church of God.

By this we know that we love the children of God, because we love God. How is this so? Aren't the children of God and God himself two different things? But one who loves God loves his commandments. And what are his commandments? "A new commandment I give you, that you love one another." You can't excuse yourselves from one love because of another. This love holds together! As it is itself joined together in one, so it makes all those who depend on it one single being. It fuses them together the way fire fuses gold into one lump. But unless the flame of love is kindled, the fusion of many into one can't happen.

23. Fulfillment of the Law (1 John 5:2–3)

And how can we recognize that we love the children of God? It's *because we love God and observe his commandments.* In this matter we groan from the difficulty of observing God's commandment. But listen to what I'm going to say. When do you feel oppressed? When you love what? Avarice! You have hard work in loving that. But it's no work at all to love God. Avarice will impose hardships, danger, chafing, and trouble on you, and you'll submit to it. And why? To fill your coffers you'll lose your peace of mind! Surely you were more at peace before you began to grow rich. See what avarice has imposed on you: you've filled your house and have thieves to fear; you've gained money and lost sleep. Look what avarice has commanded you: Do this—and you did it. What order has God given you? Love me. "You're fond of money," he says. "You'll seek it and often you won't find it. But if there are any who seek me, I am with them. You love honors, but you may not attain them. Are there any who loved me and didn't attain me? You want a protector or a powerful friend, and you try to get one by means of some lesser person; instead love me." This is what God is telling you: "You don't have to approach me through anyone else. Love itself makes me present to you."

Is anything sweeter than this love, my friends? Surely the psalmist is right: "The ungodly have told me of delights; but they are not as your law, O Lord." God's law is his commandment, that new commandment which is called new because it renews: "A new commandment I give you, that you love one another." See that this is really God's law. The Apostle tells us to "bear one another's burdens, and thus fulfill the law of Christ." Love is the consummation of all our works. This is our aim: it's both why we run and what we are running toward. When we've reached it we shall have rest.

For this is the love of God, that we keep his commandments. You've already heard that "on these two commandments depend all the law and the prophets." Do you see how God doesn't want to spread your attention over many pages? "On these two commandments": "You shall love the Lord your God with all your heart, and with all your soul, and with all your mind" and "You shall love your neighbor as yourself." These are the commandments this whole letter is talking about. Hold fast to love and be at peace. Why are you afraid of harming someone? Who harms any beloved person? Love, and you can't help doing good.

Do you have to rebuke someone? Love does it, not severity. Do you strike someone? It's for discipline's sake that you do it, because love of love doesn't allow you to leave anyone undisciplined. And sometimes there may be these different and contrary results: that hatred adopts pleasing ways, while love is severe. Take people who hate their enemies but feign friendship for them. When they see them doing wrong they praise them; they desire their ruin, to see them go blindly over the precipice of their wicked desires from which they may never return. They praise them, as the psalm says, "for the sinner is praised for the desires of his soul." They cover them with adulation. You see how they can hate and praise. Others seeing their friends doing similar things call them back, and if they don't listen they use words of reproof. They denounce and even prosecute them; sometimes it goes that far. Do you see how hatred may flatter and love prosecute? But don't consider the flatterer's words or the seeming severity of the other's. Look for their source, for the root from which they come. The flatterer wants to deceive, the other prosecutes in order to set straight.

My friends, it's not for me to enlarge your hearts. Ask God that you may love one another. You are to love everyone, even your enemies, not because they're already your sisters and brothers but so that they'll become so. Then you will always be aflame with love—for one who is already a sister or brother, or for your enemies, because love will make them your sisters and brothers. Whenever you love a sister or brother, you love a friend, one with you now, already bound to you in catholic unity. If you live well, you will love a sister or brother made from an enemy. But if you love someone who doesn't believe in Christ yet or who believes in him with a demon's faith, you must reprove this foolishness. You must love, and with a sister or brother's love. They are not yet your sisters and brothers, but you love them to make them so. And so all of our love is love for Christians, love for all of Christ's members. The discipline of love, dear friends, its vigor, its flowers, its fruit, its beauty, its charm, its nourishment, its drink, its food, its embraces—we can never have too much of these! If love delights us so much now when we are pilgrims, how we shall rejoice when we are in our own land!

24. Fragments
(1 John 5:8, 16, 20)

I. I don't want you to make any mistake about the passage in the letter of John the apostle where he says, *There are three witnesses, the spirit, the water, and the blood; and the three are one.* You might be tempted to say that spirit, water, and blood are three different substances, but he says that *the three are one.* Accordingly, I'm giving you this warning. He is speaking here of sacraments, mysteries. In things of this kind you must always pay attention to what they reveal, not to what they are. Because they are signs or images of realities, what they are in themselves is one thing and what they mean is another. So if we comprehend what is meant by these things, we do find them to be of one substance. It's as if we should say that the rock and the water are one, meaning by the rock Christ and by the water the Holy Spirit. No one can doubt that rock and water are two different elements, but because Christ and the Holy Spirit are of one and the same nature, when someone says that the rock and the water are one, it can correctly be taken in the following sense: two things who natures are different are the signs of two other things whose nature is one.

We know that the three things mentioned in the text issued from the Lord's body while he hung on the cross. First there was his spirit: "And he bowed his head and gave up his spirit." Then, when his side was pierced by the spear, "there came out blood and water." If we look at these three things in them-

---

Translator's note: Several passages from Augustine's works, in which he discusses three lines from John's first letter not covered in the homilies, were added by the translator of the Nicene and post-Nicene Fathers edition. Some of these (in new translations) have been included here. The sources of these six passages are provided in the notes at the end of the volume.

selves, we see that each has its own distinct substance; therefore they are not one. But if we want to inquire into the meaning of each of them, not unreasonably the Trinity comes to our minds. The Trinity is the one, sole, true, supreme God, Father and Son and Holy Spirit. We can say of it with perfect truth that *there are three witnesses . . . and the three are one.* Therefore we can take *spirit* to signify God the Father. It was about worshiping him that the Lord was speaking when he said that "God is spirit." By *blood* we signify the Son, because "the Word became flesh." By *water* we mean the Holy Spirit. When Jesus was talking about the *water* to be given to those who thirst, the Evangelist observed that "this he said about the Spirit which those who believed in him were to receive." And who that believes the gospel can doubt that the Father, the Son, and the Holy Spirit are *witnesses?* It is the Son who says, "I am one who bears witness to myself; and the Father who sent me bears witness to me." Although he doesn't mention the Holy Spirit here, this doesn't mean that he is separated from them. In another place he shows clearly enough that the Spirit too is a witness, saying that "he will bear witness to me." Here we have *three witnesses . . . and the three are one,* because they are of one substance.

But because the three signs by which the three Persons are signified issued from the Lord's body, they symbolized the Church as it preaches the Trinity, indicating that it has one and the same nature. This is because these Three that are signified in a threefold manner are One, and the Church which preaches them is Christ's body. If then the three things by which they are signified came forth from the Lord's body, so too did the words commanding that all nations be baptized "in the name of the Father and of the Son and of the Holy Spirit." "In the name," Jesus said, not "the names," for these *three are one* and the one God is these Three.

If this deep mystery that we read in John's letter can be explained and comprehended in some other way that is still in conformity with our catholic faith, neither combining nor di-

viding the Trinity, neither denying the Three Persons nor be-
lieving them to be of different substances, we should not reject
it for any reason. We should be glad if anything in Holy Scripture that is expressed obscurely for the purpose of exercising
the minds of the faithful can be explained in more than one
way, provided it is explained wisely.

II. *If anyone knows that his brother is committing a sin that is not
unto death he will ask and the Lord will give life to him whose sin is
not unto death; but there is a sin unto death; I do not say that one is to
pray for that.* These words of the apostle John clearly show that
there are some sisters and brothers we are instructed not to pray
for. Yet our Lord commands us to pray even for our persecutors. This difficulty can be resolved only if we admit that there
are some sins among brethren that are worse than persecution
by our enemies. That *brethren* means Christians is shown by
many texts in Scripture, of which the clearest is this one of the
Apostle: "For the unbelieving husband is sanctified in his wife,
and the unbelieving wife is sanctified in her brother." He
didn't add *our,* but considered it clear that by *brother* he meant a
Christian who had an unbelieving wife. Accordingly he goes
on: "But if the unbeliever departs, let it be so: in such cases the
brother or sister is not bound."

Therefore I take it that a sin of sisters or brothers is *unto death*
when, after they have come to know God through the grace of
our Lord Jesus Christ, they fight against the community and
are inflamed by malice to attack the very grace by which they
are reconciled to God. They commit a *sin . . . not unto death*
when through some weakness of soul they fail to perform the
community services required of them, but without withdraw-
ing their love from their sisters and brothers. The Lord, on the
cross, said, "Father, forgive them, for they know not what they
do," because they hadn't yet become sharers in the grace of the
Holy Spirit and entered the holy community. And Saint Stephen, in the Acts of the Apostles, prayed for those who were
stoning him, because they hadn't yet come to believe in Christ
and weren't fighting against a grace they shared with others.

Also, in my opinion, the reason the apostle Paul did not pray for Alexander was that he was a brother and had sinned unto death by attacking the community out of envy. He did pray for the forgiveness of those who hadn't broken the bonds of love but had given in to their fear. This is what he says: "Alexander the coppersmith did me much harm; the Lord will requite him for his deeds. Beware of him yourself, for he strongly opposed our message." Then he shows whom he does pray for, saying, "At my first defense no one took my part, but they all deserted me. May it not be charged against them!"

Therefore the Lord's precept that we love our enemies, do good to those who hate us, and pray for those who persecute us may be taken to mean that for some sins, even of our sisters and brothers, we are not commanded to pray. Otherwise my ignorance may make holy Scripture seem self-contradictory, which it cannot be. But as there are some for whom we are not to pray, are there others we are to pray against, as we read in certain psalms? In general, this is what is said: "Bless and do not curse" and "Repay no one evil for evil." Not praying for someone is not praying against that one. You can see that their punishment is certain and their salvation utterly hopeless. So the reason you do not pray for them is not because you hate them, but because you feel you can do them no good. Further, you do not want your prayer rejected by the most just Judge.

III. Such is the liberty they receive by this grace, namely, that although as long as they are living here below they have to fight against sinful desires and are overcome by some sins (this is why they pray everyday, "Forgive us our debts"), yet they no longer serve the sin *unto death* of which John says, *There is a sin unto death; I do not say that one is to pray for that.* Because John doesn't tell us what this sin is, many different opinions can be held. It is my opinion that this sin is the abandonment all the way up to death of "the faith that works by love."

IV. We read in Scripture the words, *that we may be in his true Son Jesus Christ; he is the true God and eternal life.* We must yield to such weighty evidence. Tell me then whether this *true Son* of God—who is distinguished by this word *true* from those who are children of God by grace—is of no substance or of some substance? You answer, "I don't say that he is of no substance, lest I say that he is of nothing. Therefore he is of some substance." And I ask you, "Of what substance? If he's not of the Father's substance, then you have to find another. If you don't—and you don't—then acknowledge that he is of the Father's substance and confess that the Son is *homousion,* of one substance, with the Father."

V. As you speak of an unbegotten Father, I profess a Son who was begotten. But because one is unbegotten and the other begotten, they are not therefore of different natures and substances. Certainly if one is begotten, he is a Son. If he is a Son, he is a *true Son* because he is only-begotten. For we are also called sons, but are we who are so many only-begotten? He is an only-begotten Son in another way: he is son by nature, we by grace. He is the only-begotten of the Father. He is what the Father is with respect to nature and substance. Anyone who says that because he is begotten he is of another nature denies that he is a *true Son.* But we read in Scripture *that we may be in his true Son Jesus Christ; he is the true God and eternal life.* Why is he *the true God?* It's because he is the *true Son* of God. If by God's gift animals beget only their own kind, humans begetting humans and dogs begetting dogs, shouldn't God beget God?

Thus if the Son is of the same substance as the Father, why do you call him less than the Father? Is it because when a human father begets a son, even though they are both human beings, it is a greater who begets a lesser? Should we expect Christ to grow up, then, as humans begotten by humans do? But if Christ, ever since he was begotten (which was not in time but from eternity), is what he is and yet is less than the Father, as you say, then the human condition is preferable. Humans can grow and sooner or later come to the age and the strength of their fathers, but he never can do the same. How is he then a *true Son?*

VI. Those who have said that our Lord Jesus Christ is not God, or is not the true God, or is not the one and only God with the Father, or is not truly immortal because he is mutable are convicted of their error by the clear and unanimous voice of holy Scripture where it says, "In the beginning was the Word, and the Word was with God, and the Word was God." Evidently we accept this "Word of God" as God's only Son, of whom Scripture says shortly after, "And the Word was made flesh, and dwelt among us" because of his birth in flesh, which took place in time from the Virgin.

But John is asserting here not only that he is God but also that he is of the same substance as the Father. Having said "and the Word was God," he adds that "he was in the beginning with God; all things were made through him and without him nothing was made." He does not say "all things" simply but "all things were made." That is every creature, and so clearly he through whom all things were made was not made. If he was not made, then he is not a creature. If he is not a creature, he is of the same substance as the Father. Every substance which is not God is a creature; what is not a creature is God. If the Son is not of the same substance as the Father, then he is a created substance. If this is true, then everything was not made through him. Yet "all things were made through him," and therefore he is of one and the same substance as the Father and is not only God but even *the true God.* The same writer says this with great clarity in his letter: *We know that the Son of God has come and has given us understanding that we may come to know the true God and may be in his true Son Jesus Christ; he is the true God and eternal life.*

Notes

INTRODUCTION

p. v "**up to his . . . .**" Roy J. Deferrari, ed., *Early Christian Biographies,* vol. 1 of *The Fathers of the Church* series (Washington, D.C.: Catholic University Press, 1952), p. 123.

viii "**Augustine's exegesis is . . .**" *Augustine: Later Works,* vol. VIII of *The Library of Christian Classics* (Philadelphia; Westminister, 1980), p. 258.

ix "**for Augustine, it . . .**" vol. 1 of *The Cambridge History of the Bible* (Cambridge, 1970), p. 547.

"**It is the . . .**" *De Doctrina Christiana,* IV, 4, 6.

1. THE INCARNATION (Homily 1, 1–3)

p. 1 "**In the beginning . . .**" John 1:1.
"**men have eaten . . .**" Ps. 77:25 (Latin) = 78:25 (Hebrew)*
"**The Word became . . .**" John 1:14.
"**he placed his . . .**" Ps. 18:6=19:4–5.
2 "**everything was made . . .**" John 1:3.
"**they shall be . . .**" Gen. 2:24.
"**they are . . .**" Matt. 19:6.
"**He has wreathed . . .**" Isa. 61:10.
"**One of the . . .**" John 20:26–29.

2. WALK IN THE LIGHT (Homily 1, 4–8)

p. 5 "**Draw near to . . .**" Ps. 33:6=34:5.
"**what communion . . .**" 2 Cor. 6:14.
"**the devil and . . .**" Eph. 6:12.
6 "**bond of . . .**" Col. 2:14.
7 "**Love buries . . .**" 1 Peter 4:8.
"**Turn away your . . .**" Ps. 50:11=51:9.
"**For I know . . .**" Ps. 50:5=51:3.
"**Every person . . .**" Rom. 3:4.
9 "**Pray for us . . .**" Col. 4:3.
"**Lo, here is . . .**" Matt. 24:23.
"**we have found . . .**" Ps. 131:6=132:6.
"**that mountain which . . .**" Dan. 2:35.

3. THE COMMANDMENT OF LOVE (Homily 1, 9–13)

p. 10 "**A new commandment . . .**" John 13:34.
11 "**Forgive them, for . . .**" Luke 23:34.

---

* Throughout these notes, references to the Psalms will follow this format: first the Latin number will be given, then the Hebrew.

11 **"Be perfect, therefore ... "** Matt. 5:48.
"You have put ... " Col. 3:9–10.
"Once you were ... " Eph. 5:8.
12 **"Great peace have ... "** Ps. 118:165=119:165.
"forbearing one another ... " Eph. 4:2–3.
"Bear one another's ... " Gal. 6:2.
13 **"stone cut out ... "** Dan. 2:34.
"the promise made ... " Gen. 22:18.
"A city set ... " Matt. 5:14.

4. I AM WRITING TO YOU (Homily 2, 4–8)

p. 14 **"Was it Paul ... "** 1 Cor. 1:13.
"all things were ... " John 1:3.
15 **"Before Abraham was ... "** John 8:58.
"your years shall ... " Ps. 101:28=102:27.
"Today I have ... " Ps. 2:7.
"You shall tell ... " Exod. 3:14.
"Before the daystar ... " Ps. 109.3=110:3.
"everything was made ... " John 1:3.
"that which is ... " 1 John 1:1.
"the Beginning ... " John 8:25.
16 **"He was crucified ... "** 2 Cor. 13:4.
"Knowledge puffs up ... " 1 Cor. 8:1.
"The demons acknowledged ... " Matt. 8:29.

5. TWO LOVES (Homily 2, 8–14)

p. 18 **"power of religion ... "** 2 Tim. 3:5.
"rooted and grounded ... " Eph. 3:17.
19 **"they worshipped and ... "** Rom. 1:25.
21 **"Do not rejoice ... "** Luke 10:20.
"certain false prophets ... " Matt. 24:24.
"the Lord was tempted ... " Matt. 4:1– 11.
22 **"I have said ... "** Ps. 81:6=82:6.

6. CHRIST AND THE ANTICHRISTS (Homily 3, 1–10)

p. 24 **"is born of ... "** John 3:5.
"In the beginning ... " John 1:1.
"Do not touch ... " John 20:17.
"Put your finger ... " John 20:27.
25 **"Have I been ... "** John 14:9.
26 **"If one member ... "** 1 Cor. 12:26.
28 **"I am the ... "** John 14:6.
"a great mountain ... " Dan. 2:35.
"Whoever stumbles ... " Luke 20:18.
29 **"they profess to ... "** Titus 1:16.
"You hypocrites, how ... " Matt. 12:34.
"figs from thistles ... " Matt. 7:16.
30 **"the hymn the ... "** Dan. chapter 3.

7. THE SPIRITUAL ANOINTING (Homilies 3, 11–13; 4, 2–3)

p. 32 "For the sake . . . " Ps. 16:4 = 17:4.
33 "Come, blessed of . . . " Matt. 25:34.
"Go into the . . . " Matt. 25:41.
34 "Call no one . . . " Matt. 23:10.
35 "I planted, Apollos . . . " 1 Cor. 3:6–7.
"Go, preach the . . . " Mark 16:15.
36 "If you abide . . . " John 8:31– 32.
"He who promised . . . " Heb. 10:23.
54 "Begin to make . . . " Ps. 146:7 after the Septuagint.
"when death is . . . " 1 Cor. 15:54.
37 "You have spoken . . . " Job 2:10.

8. LIVING AS CHILDREN OF GOD (Homily 4, 4– 7)

p. 39 "In the beginning . . . " John 1:1.
"who, though he . . . " Phil. 2:6.
"cursed be all . . . " Jer. 17:5.
"They shall look . . . " John 19:37.
40 "Come, blessed of . . . " Matt. 25:34.
"Go into the . . . " Matt. 25:41.
"Blessed are the . . . " Matt. 5:8.
"which no eye . . . " 1 Cor. 2:9.
41 "Not that I . . . " Phil. 3:12–14.
"By hope we . . . " Rom. 8:24–25.
42 "Be my helper . . . " Ps. 26:9 = 27:9.

9. AVOIDING SIN (Homilies 4, 8–12; 5, 1–6)

p. 43 "We walk by . . . " 2 Cor. 5:7.
"the righteous man . . . " Rom. 1:17.
44 "They were Abraham's . . . " John 8:37.
45 "If we say . . . " 1 John 1:8.
46 "A new commandment . . . " John 13:34.
"Love buries a . . . " 1 Peter 4:8.
"Father, forgive them . . . " Luke 23:34.
"Lord, do not . . . " Acts 7:59 (60).
"I myself will . . . " 2 Cor. 12:15.
"Paul was among . . . " Acts 8:1.
47 "To me to . . . " Phil. 1:21, 23–24.
"If I know . . . " 1 Cor. 13:2.

10. THE LAW OF LOVE (Homily 5, 7–13)

p. 48 "If we say . . . " 1 John 1:8.
"one who hates . . . " 1 John 2:11.
"For I have . . . " 1 Cor. 4:15.
49 "One who loves . . . " Rom. 13:8.
"Love is the . . . " Rom. 13:10.
"the pearl the . . . " Matt. 13:45–46.

50 "Love is not . . . " 1 Cor. 13:4.
"the world was . . . " John 1:10.
"He is the . . . " 1 John 2:2.
51 "Greater love no . . . " John 15:13.

11. TRUE LOVE (Homily 6, 1–4)

p. 54 "Greater love no . . . " John 15:13.
"As he laid . . . " 1 John 3:16.
"If anyone has . . . " 1 John 3:17.
55 "I will myself . . . " 2 Cor. 12:15.
"For me it is . . . " 1 Cor. 4:3.
"If I give . . . " 1 Cor. 13:3.
"For our boast . . . " 2 Cor. 1:12.
"But let each . . . " Gal. 6:4.
56 "Beware of practicing . . . " Matt. 6:1.
"do not let . . . " Matt. 6:3.
"Where shall I . . . " Ps. 138:7 = 139:7.
"If I ascend . . . " Ps. 138:8 = 139:8.
"You are my . . . " Ps. 31:7 = 32:7.
57 "A new commandment . . . " John 13:34.

12. UNANSWERED PRAYER (Homily 6, 5–8)

p. 58 "Lest I be . . . " 2 Cor. 12:7–9.
60 "God gave them . . . " Rom. 1:24.
"We do not . . . " Rom. 8:26–27.
"God's love has . . . " Rom. 5:5.

13. FAITH AND LOVE (Homily 6, 9–13)

p. 62 "God's love has . . . " Rom. 5:5.
"If our hearts . . . " 1 John 3:21.
"they would speak . . . " Acts 2:4.
64 "If anyone thirst . . . " John 7:37–39.
"Keep far from . . . " Prov. 9:18 after the Septuagint.
"in the book . . . " Rev. 17:15.
"Counsel is a . . . " Prov. 16:22.
65 "They went out . . . " 1 John 2:19.
66 "they profess to . . . " Titus 1:16.
"In the beginning . . . " John 1:1.
"without leaving heaven . . . " John 3:13.
"Greater love than . . . " John 15:13.
"these earthen vessels . . . " 2 Cor. 4:7.

14. GOD IS LOVE (Homily 7, 2–6)

p. 68 "Greater love than . . . " John 15:13.
69 "If you forgive . . . " Matt. 6:14–15.
"I am the . . . " John 14:6.
"Father, forgive them . . . " Luke 23:34.
70 "God is love . . . " On this text see also Augustine, *De Trinitate*, VIII, 8(12).

"God's love has ... " Rom. 5:5.
"Let your fountain ... " Prov. 5:16–17.
71 "King Saul had ... " 1 Samuel 19.
"anyone who eats ... " 1 Cor. 11:29.
"they defiled the ... " Ezek. 36:20.

15. GOD HAS LOVED US FIRST (Homily 7, 7–11)

p. 72 "Greater love than ... " John 15:13.
"He who did ... " Rom. 8:32.
"the Son of ... " Gal. 2:20.
73 "Peter, do you ... " John 21:15– 17.
74 "Blessed are the ... " Matt. 5:8.
"God is love ... " 1 John 4:8.
"Blessed is he ... " Ps. 40:2 = 41:1.
"He who has ... " Luke 8:8.
75 "the dove that ... " Matt. 3:16.
76 "whom your parents ... " Heb. 12:7.

16. CARING FOR LOVE (Homily 8, 1–3)

p. 77 "inner self ... " Eph. 3:16.
"In our hearts ... " Eph. 3:17.
78 "Beware of practicing ... " Matt. 6:1.

17. LOVE OF OUR ENEMIES (Homily 8, 4–10)

p. 80 "one who loves ... " 1 John 2:10.
"This is his ... " 1 John 3:23.
"For if you ... " Matt. 5:46.
82 "I wish that ... " 1 Cor. 7:7 (the sense here is quite different from Saint Paul's).
83 "those who are ... " Matt. 9:12.
"to love our enemies ... " Matt. 5:44.
"Father, forgive them ... " Luke 23:34.

18. ABIDING IN GOD (Homily 8, 12–14)

p. 84 "Because God's love ... " Rom. 5:5.
"For in hope ... " Rom. 8:24.
"this corruptible nature ... " 1 Cor. 15:53.
85 "I have said ... " Ps. 15:2 = 16:2.
"One sheep strayed ... " Luke 15:4–5.

19. CONFIDENCE FOR THE DAY OF JUDGMENT (Homily 9, 1–3)

p. 87 "I became little ... " 1 Thess. 2:7.
88 "The fear of ... " Prov. 1:7; Sirach 1:16; Ps. 110:10 = 111:10.
"members which are ... " Col. 3:5.
"the spiritual hosts ... " Eph. 6:12.
"thy kingdom come! ... " Matt. 6:10.
89 "And you, O ... " Ps. 6:4–5 = 6:3–4.

"to depart and ... " Phil. 1:23-24.
90 "If you love ... " Matt. 5:44-46.

20. LOVE CASTS OUT FEAR (Homily 9, 4-8)

p. 91 "the fear of ... " Prov. 1:7, and so on.
"Who will separate ... " Rom. 8:35.
"And who is ... " 1 Peter 3:13.
92 "You have turned ... " Ps. 29:12- 13=30:11-12.
"If you are ... " Sirach 1:28.
"The fear of ... " Ps. 18:10=19:9.
94 "to turn his ... " Ps. 50:11=51:9.
"because I know ... " Ps. 50:5=51:3.
95 "I come": Rev. 22:20.
"I will sing ... " Ps. 100:1-2=101:1-2.

21. GOD FIRST LOVED US (Homily 9, 9-11)

p. 96 "But God shows ... " Rom. 5:8.
97 "You are the ... " Ps. 44:3=45:2.
"in the beginning ... " John 1:1.
"And we saw ... " Is. 53:2.
"Though he was ... " Phil. 2:6.
"But he emptied ... " Phil. 2:7-8.
"that pure fear ... " Ps. 18:10=19:9.
98 "God is love ... " 1 John 4:8, 16.
"You have destroyed ... " Ps. 72:27=73:27.
"But for me ... " Ps. 72:28=73:28.
99 "anyone who hates ... " 1 John 3:15.
"that we love ... " 1 John 3:23.
"A new commandment ... " John 13:34.

22. ONE CHRIST, LOVING HIMSELF (Homily 10, 1-3)

p. 100 "faith that works ... " Gal. 5:6.
"the demons believe ... " James 2:19.
"we know who ... " Matt. 8:29.
"You are the ... " Matt. 16:16.
101 "If one member ... " 1 Cor. 12:26.
"Now you are ... " 1 Cor. 12:27.
102 "He who does ... " 1 John 4:20.
"Saul, Saul ... " Acts 9:4.
"A new commandment ... " John 13:34.

23. FULFILLMENT OF THE LAW (Homily 10, 4 and 7)

p. 103 "The ungodly have ... " Ps. 118:85=119:85.
"A new commandment ... " John 13:34.
"bear one another's ... " Gal. 6:2.
"on these two ... " Matt. 22:37- 40.
104 "for the sinner ... " Ps. 9:3=10:3.

24. FRAGMENTS

I. *Contra Maximinum Arianorum Episcopum*, II, 22, 3.

p. 106 **"And he bowed ... "** John 19:30.

"there came out ... " John 19:34.

107 **"God is spirit ... "** John 4:24.

"the Word became ... " John 1:14.

"this he said ... " John 7:39.

"I am one ... " John 8:18.

"he will bear ... " John 15:26.

"in the name ... " Matt. 28:19.

II. *De Sermone Domini in Monte*, I, 22, 73–76.

108 **"our Lord commands ... "** Matt. 5:44.

"For the unbelieving ... " 1 Cor. 7:14–15.

"Father, forgive them ... " Luke 23:34.

"Saint Stephen in ... " Acts 7:59 (60).

109 **"Alexander the coppersmith ... "** 2 Tim. 4:14–16.

"in certain psalms ... " Ps. 68=69, 108=109.

"Bless and do ... " Rom. 12:14.

"Repay no one ... " Rom. 12:17.

III. *Liber de Corruptione et Gratia*, 35.

"Forgive us our ... " Matt. 6:12.

"the faith that ... " Gal. 5:6.

IV. *Contra Maximinum Arianorum Episcopum*, II, 14, 3.

V. *Collatio cum Maximino Arianorum Episcopo*, 14.

VI. *De Trinitate*, I, 6, 9.

111 **"In the beginning ... "** John 1:1.

"And the Word ... " John 1:14.

"he was in ... " John 1:2–3.